Jake Walton
SUNLIGHT AND SHADE
Celtic Song Affairs

AF287211

Jake Walton

SUNLIGHT AND SHADE
Celtic Song Affairs

Illustrationen

Vivien Nicholson

Song Bücherei

Erste Auflage / First Edition 2014
Copyright © Heupferd Musik Verlag GmbH, Dreieich
Alle Rechte vorbehalten / All rights reserved
Die Song Bücherei wird herausgegeben von
Christian Winkelmann
und erscheint im Heupferd Musik Verlag
www.heupferd-musik.de
Transkriptionen von John Davison
Fotos von Kirsten Claire, Ed Davis & Mike Wigg
Umschlag, Satz, Layout & Übersetzungen von Y & M
Printed in Germany
ISBN 978-3-923445-11-0

Contents / Inhalt

Intro

by Jez Lowe

Jake Walton was already a name familiar to me, with a reputation as a tasteful instrumentalist and singer of fine songs, before our paths finally crossed at Pontardawe Folk Festival in the hot summer of 1980. There we began a friendship and partnership that has endured ever since, and I continue to follow keenly his unique and enthralling musical path through life to this day.

This collection of songs delve deep into his repertoire, and include some of the evocative traditional ballads and modern folksongs that have inspired him, as well as a choice pick of his own compositions, many of which have in turn inspired others, including myself. Jake and I have travelled the world together over the years, and it's good that he has taken time out to bring this collection of songs together, as a fond salute to the singers of the past, and a rich source of the singers of the future.

Jake Walton war mir schon als einfühlsamer Instrumentalist und Sänger längst ein Begriff, bevor sich unsere Wege schliesslich im heißen Sommer des Jahres auf dem Pontardawe Folk Festival kreuzten. Dort begann unsere innige Freund- und Parterschaft, die bis heute andauert. Und ich werde seinen einzigartigen und verzaubernden musikalischen Pfaden auch künftig folgen.

Diese Liedersammlung ergründet alle Aspekte seines Repertoires und umfasst einige der beziehungsreichsten traditionellen Balladen und zeitgenössischen Folksongs, die ihn berührt haben. Ebenso eine Auswahl seiner eigenen Werke, viele davon haben mich und andere stark inspiriert. Jake und ich sind im Verlauf der Jahre viel herumgekommen und er hat gut daran getan, diese Sammlung ins Werk zu setzen. Als liebevolle Remineszenz an die Liedersänger der Vergangeheit und als ergiebige Quelle künftiger Sängergenerationen.

The Music Makers

Words: Arthur O'Shaughnessy; Adapted: Jake Walton
Music: Jake Walton

Arthur O'Shaughnessy (1844 – 1881) was born in London and wrote several books and poems, including some for children. He was also involved in the Pre-Raphaelite movement. I have altered his poem somewhat and sing it to the souls of the old minstrels and troubadours as an invocation for their inspiration.

Arthur O'Shaughnessy (1844 – 1881) wurde in London geboren. Bis zu seinem Tod hat er zahlreiche Bücher und Gedichte verfasst, einige davon für Kinder. Er war auch in der Bewegung der Prä-Raphaeliten engagiert. Ich habe sein Gedicht etwas umgearbeitet und singe es zu Ehren der alten Minstrelsänger u

Guit. tuning: EADGAE

We are the mu - sic ma - kers,___ and we are the

dream-ers of dreams,___ wan-der-ing___ by lone

sea break-ers,___ or sit-ting___ by de - so-late streams,

world los-ers and world for - sa - kers, on

which the pale moon___ gleams, yet

we are___ the mo - vers___ and sh - a - kers,

9

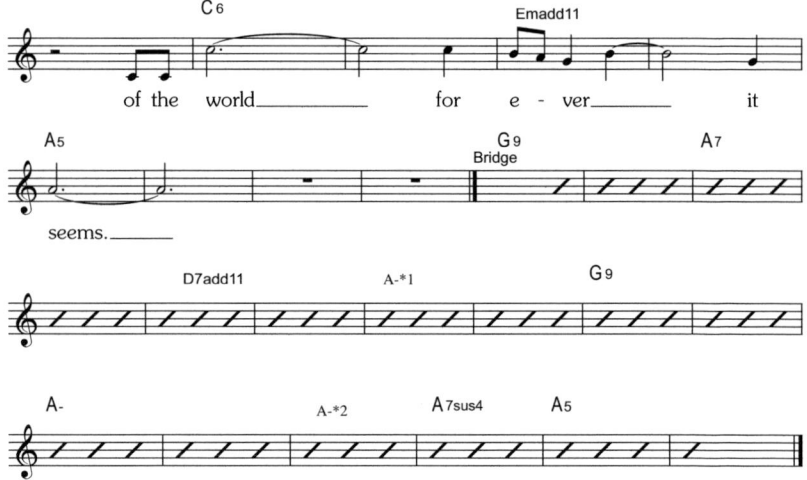

of the world_____ for e - ver_____ it seems._____

We are the music makers,
And we are the dreamers of dreams,
Wandering by lone sea-breakers,
Or sitting by desolate streams,
World losers and world-forsakers,
On which the pale moon gleams,
Yet we are the movers and shakers,
Of the world forever it seems.

Oh hail we cry to the comers,
From the dazzling unknown shore,
Bring hither your sun and your summers,
Renew our world as of yore,
You shall teach us your songs new numbers,
And things we've dreamed not before,
In spite of a dreamer who slumbers,
And a singer who sings no more.

Yet you with your dreaming and singing,
Ceaseless and sorrowless be,
The glory around you clinging,
Of the glorious future you see,
Your souls with the high music ringing,
Oh must it forever be,

You'll dwell in your dreaming and singing,
Too far apart for us to see.

And we are the music makers,
And we are the dreamers of dreams.

The Gloaming Grey (My Ain Kind Dearie' O)

Words: Robert Burns; Music: trad., arr. Jake Walton

The famous Scottish poet Robert Burns (1759 – 1796) reworked this poem
from an older Scottish one. It has been set to the traditional tune „The Lea
Rigs" which is usually played as a fast dance tune, however slowed down it
makes a haunting melody for this beautiful poem. I used his description of
twilight as „The Gloaming Grey" for te title of my first solo LP in the late
1970's.

Der berühmte schottische Dichter Robert Burns (1759 – 1796) hat seine Verse nach einer älteren schottischen Fassung dieses Gedichts verfasst. Sie wurden mit der traditionellen Melodie „The Lea Rigs" vertont, welche eigentlich
als schneller Tanz gespielt worden ist, hier jedoch etwas verlangsamt eine kon-
geniale Melodie für dieses wunderschöne Gedicht abgibt. Ich verwendete in
den späten 70ern seine Beschreibung der Dämmerung als Titelsong für meine
erste LP „The Gloaming Grey".

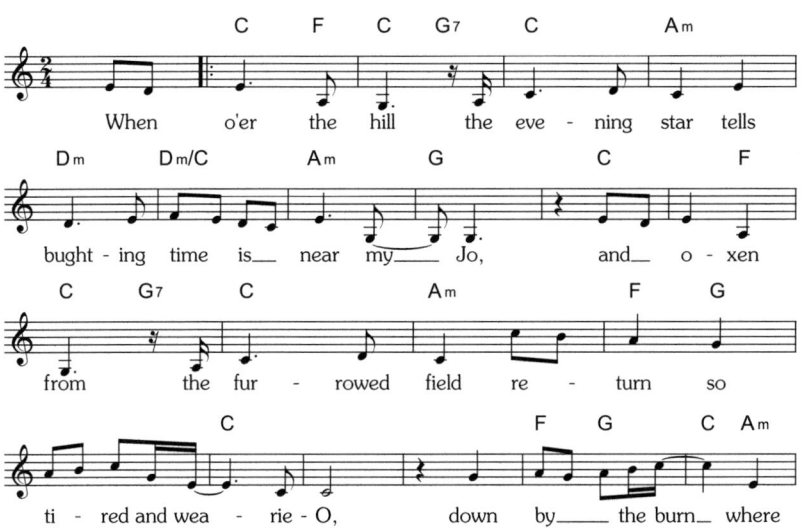

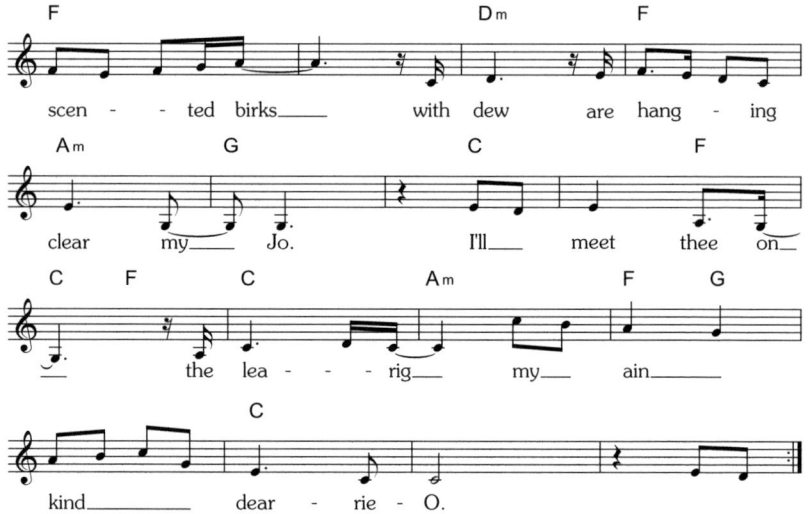

When o'er the hill the evening star tells bughting time is near me Jo,
And oxen from the furrowed field return so tired and wearie-O,
Down by the burn where scented birks with dew are hanging clear my Jo,
I'll meet thee on the lea-rig my ain kind dearie-O.

In mirkest glen at midnight hour I'd rove and ne'er be eerie-O,
If through that glen I gaed to thee my kind dearie-O,
Although the night we ne'er sae wild and I were ne'er so wearie-O,
I'd meet thee on the lea-rig my ain kind rearie-O.

The hunter loves the morning sun to rouse the mountain deer my Jo,
At noon the fisher seeks the glen along the burn to steer my Jo,
But give me the hour of the gloaming grey it makes my heart so cheery-O,
To meet thee on the lea-rig my ain kind dearie-O.

After The Plough

Words: Elizabeth J. Coatsworth
Music: Jake Walton

The sight of seagulls following the plough is a common one in the south west of England. This evocative old Cornish poem captures for me the reflective moods of autumn. I remember using the Dulcimer to accompany it after setting it to this melody in the 1970's.

Der Anblick von Seemöwen, die dem Pflug folgen, ist im Südwesten Englans allgegenwärtig. Dieses alte gehaltvolle Gedicht aus Cornwall verkörpert für mich die nachdenkliche Stimmung des Herbstes. Seit ich es in den 1970ern mit dieser Melodie vertont habe, verwende ich zur Begleitung den Dulcimer.

13

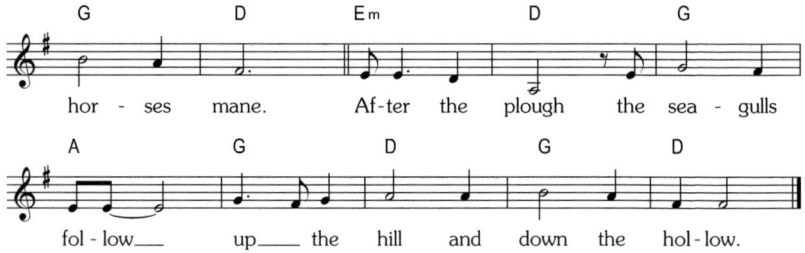

hor - ses mane. Af-ter the plough the sea - gulls fol - low___ up___ the hill and down the hol - low.

After the plough the seagulls follow
Up the hill and down the hollow.
A cloud of wings, a storm of cries,
They rise and fall, they fall and rise.

The slow brown furrow rolls from the share,
The seagulls hover their pale eyes stare.
And the ploughman dreams of his youth again,
A high dark wave and a horses mane.

After the plough the seagulls follow
Up the hill and down the hollow

The Bonny Labouring Boy

Words: trad.
Music: trad., arr. Jake Walton

When I first started to learn and listen to „traditional" songs it seemed as if they invariably started with somebody „walking out one morning in spring". After awhile this started to somewhat lose its appeal for me! However this song proved to be an exception and I have never tired of its lyrical melody. I believe I first heard it sung by Sean Cannon, a very fine singer, many years before he joined the Dubliners. It is also often known as „The Bonny Irish Boy" and may be found in Coln O' Lochlainn's book „Irish Street Ballads". There are many songs with a similar theme, but in this one it seems the girl successfully defies her parents and marries the man she loves.

Als ich damit anfing, mich mit „traditionellen" Liedern zu beschäftigen, schienen sie stets damit zu beginnen, dass jemand an einem Frühlingsmorgen auszog. Mit der Zeit verlor das für mich seinen Reiz. Dieses Lied jedoch ist eine Ausnahme und ich bin seiner lyrischen Melodie nie überdrüssig geworden. Ich glaube, ich habe es zum ersten Mal von dem grossartigen Sänger Sean Cannon gehört, viele Jahre bevor er bei den Dubliners mitwirkte. Man kennt es auch als „The Bonny Irish Boy" und findet es in Colm O'Lochlainns Buch „The Irish Street Ballads". Es gibt eine Menge Lieder mit ähnlicher Thematik, aber in diesem widersetzt sich das Mädchen ihren Eltern erfolgreich und heiratet am Ende den Mann, des es liebt.

As I walked out one morning it was in the months of spring,
I heard a lovely maid complain so grievously did sing.
Saying cruel were my parents, they did me so annoy.
They would not let me marry with my bonny labouring boy.

Johnny is my true loves name as you may plainly see,
My parents did employ him their labouring boy to be.
To harrow to reap to sow the seed to plough my fathers land,
And soon I fell in love with him as you may understand.

Said the mother to her daughter: Why do you choose so low,
To marry a poor labouring boy around the world you'll go.
Some noble lord might fancy you great riches to enjoy,
So do not throw yourself away on the bonny Irish boy.

Said the daughter to her mother: Your talk is all in vain,
For Knights and Lords and Dukes and Earls their effort I disdain.
I'd sooner live a humble life where time I would employ,
Still waiting happy prospects with my bonny labouring boy.

Fill our glasses to the brim and let the toast go round,
Here's a health to every labouring boy that plough and sow the ground.
And when his work is over its home he'll go with joy,
And happy is the girl that weds the bonny labouring boy.

Lamachree And Megrum

Words: trad.
Music: trad., arr. Jake Walton

The Bothy houses in Scotland were the meeting places for workers and farm labourers and many songs were collected from them. This bothy ballad is the song of a farm worker singing to his two horses, Lamachree and Megrum as he ploughs. I first learnt it from John Bidwell who in turn heard it from the singing of Clive Palmer. It is printed in Ewan MacColl's „Folk Songs and Ballads of Scotland" although the version here I have anglicised a little and taken the liberty of adding a chorus. The melody feels as if it has come straight from the land and with the repetition of the second and fourth lines has for me a strong hypnotic effect.
Glossary:
Herb to hash and haick the loon = A meddlesome person. Sair = To serve. Fremt = The stranger. Abune = Above. Sheen = Shoes.

Bothyhouses waren in Schottland Treffpunkte von Arbeitern und Tagelöhnern, die eine Unmenge von Liedern sammelten. Diese Bothy-Ballade ist das

Lied eines Landarbeiters, das er seinen beiden Pferden Lamarchee und Megrum beim Pflügen vorsang. John Bidwell machte mich mit ihr vertraut, der sie seinerseits von Clive Palmer kannte. Sie ist in Ewan MacColl's Sammlung „Folk Songs And Ballads Of Scotland" abgedruckt, allerdings habe ich diese Fassung etwas anglisiert und mir die Freiheit genommen, einen Refrain hinzu zu fügen. Die Melodie fühlt sich an als käme sie geradewegs vom Lande und durch die Wiederholung der zweiten und vierten Zeile erzielt es eines Erachtens eine starke hypnotische Wirkung.

„Herp to hash an haick the loon" meint: eine aufdringliche Person. „Sait" meint: dienen. „Fremt" meint: Fremder. „Abune" meint: oben. Und „Sheen" meint: Schuhe.

When first I came to sair the fremt,
Lamachree and Megrum,
'T was to Auchtiedoor I skeemt,
Old grey Megrum.

Chorus:
Lullay luleiro, lullay lulleiro, lullay lullo.

The old good wife smokes the neuk,
Lamachree and Megrum,
Ordering at the throwither cook,
Old grey Megrum.

(Chorus)

The next I came to Middlethird,
Lamachree and Megrum,
A betters nae abune the yird,
Old grey Megrum.

(Chorus)

I took a turn to Middletack,
Lamachree and Megrum,
I there got meat to make me fat,
Old grey Megrum.

(Chorus)

I there got buttered bread and cheese,
Lamachree and Megrum,
And oil to keep my sheen in grease,
Old grey Megrum.

(Chorus)

I took a turn to Yokies Hill,
Lamamachree and Megrum,
The toughest place I ere gaed till,
Old grey Megrum.

(Chorus)

Aherb to hash and haick the loons,
Lamachree and Megrum,
There's nae his like in Buchan's bounds,
Old grey Megrum.

(Chorus)

19

Bogie's Bonny Belle

Words: trad.
Music: trad., arr. Jake Walton

In his book „Travellers Songs from England and Scotland" Ewan MacColl thought this song from Aberdeenshire to be of fairly recent origin, possibly later than 1925. It seems that it has been one of the most popular Bothy songs to have been collected. During the 1980's Christy Moore and Bert Jansch both recorded it and it will always remain a great favourite of mine. Heartfelt and moving storytelling at it's best, combined with its lyrical melody has established it as a standard.

In seinem Buch „Travellers Songs From England And Scotland" hält Ewan MacColl dieses Lied aus Aberdeenshire eher für jüngeren Ursprungs, möglicherweise erst nach 1925 entstanden. Es scheint wohl einer der populärsten Bothy Songs gewesen zu sein, die gesammelt worden sind. Sowohl Christy Moore als auch Bert Jansch haben es eingespielt und es wird wahrscheinlich auch mein eigener Favorit bleiben. Seine tiefsinnige und bewegende Erzählweise mit ihrer lyrischen Melodie haben es zum Standard werden lassen.

Capo 2nd Fret / Play ( ) Chords.

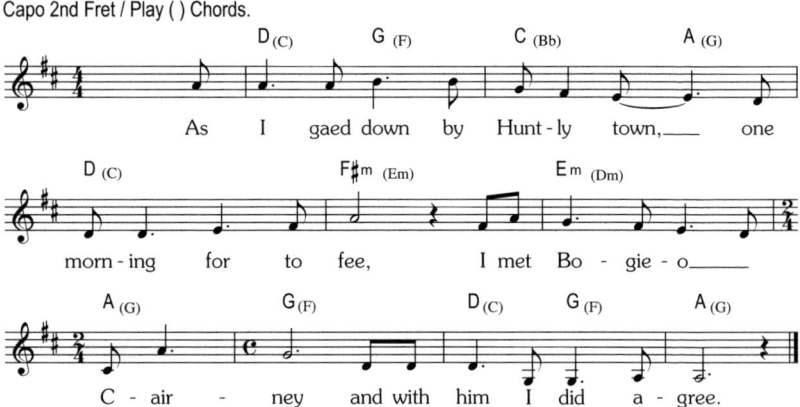

As I gaed down by Huntley town,
One morning for to fee,
I met Bogie-o' Cairnie
And with him I did agree.

To work his twa best horses,
A task that I knew well,

To work his twa best horses,
At the harrow or the plough.

Now Bogie had a daughter,
Her name was Isabel,
She was neat complete and handsome,
And sure I loved her well.

As I went out walking,
She took me for her guide,
Down by the banks o' Cairney,
To watch the small fish glide.

When three long months were gone and past,
This lass she lost her bloom,
The red fell from her rosy cheeks,
Her eyes began to swoon.

When nine long months were gone and past,
She brought to me a son,
And I was duly called for,
To see what could be done.

I said that I would marry her,
But oh no that would not do,
Saying you're no match for Isabel,
And she's no match for you.

And now she's married to a tinker lad,
Who comes from Huntley town,
Mending pots and pans and paraffin lamps,
He scours the country round.

So I'll take my young son in my arms,
And joy to him I'll give,
And perhaps he'll be as dear to me,
As the lassie I adore.

And maybe she's got the better man,
Old Bogie cana tell,
But 't was I who took the maidenhead,
Of Bogie's bonny belle.

The Gypsy's Wedding Day

Words: trad.
Music: trad., arr. Jake Walton

The musician, composer and folk song collector Percy Grainger collected this song from the Lincolnshire singer Joseph Taylor in the early 1900's. The cylinder recordings of this song and others were transferred to vinyl and released on the LP „Unto Brigg Fair" in the 1970's. This album became a big influence on the English folk revival scene and was a great favourite with singers such as Martin Carthy.

Lincolnshire is a neighbouring county to my own birthplace and this song and the others seem to capture a very English feel of the rural life at that time. I enjoyed singing this song when touring with Roger Nicholson during the 1970's and it always seemed popular with it's simple innocence and happy ending. It may even have been a true story, at least I like to think so!

Der Musiker, Komponist und Sammler von Volksliedern Percy Grainger kam in den frühen 1900ern durch den Sänger Joseph Taylor auf dieses Lied. Eine Walzenaufzeichnung dieses und anderer Lieder wurde auf Vinyl übertragen und in den 1970ern auf der LP „Unto Brigg Fair" neu veröffentlicht. Das Album hatte großen Einfluß auf die englische Folkrevival-Szene und gehörte zu den besonderen Favoriten von Sängern wie Martin Carthy.

Lincolnshire ist eine Nachbarregion meines Geburtsortes und dieser Song scheint ein sehr englisches Lebensgefühl des damaligen Landlebens zu verkörpern. Ich sang es vorzugsweise bei meinen Tourneen mit Roger Nicholson während der 1970er Jahre und es wurde mit seiner Unbedarftheit und seinem glücklichen Ausgang stets sehr gut aufgenommen. Vielleicht stimmt seine Geschichte sogar, ich hoffe es zumindest.

Guit. tuning: DGDGCD

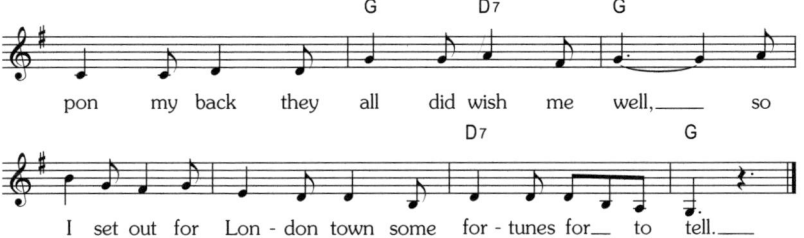

pon my back they all did wish me well,____ so

I set out for Lon - don town some for - tunes for__ to tell.____

My father is the king of the gypsies that is true,
My mother she learned me some camping for to do,
They put the pack upon my back they all did wish me well,
So I set out for London town some fortunes for to tell.

Now as I was a walking up a fair London street,
A handsome young squire I chanced for to meet,
He viewed my brown cheeks and he liked them oh so well,
He said me little gypsy girl can you me fortune tell?

Why yes kind sir give me hold of your hand,
Why you have got houses you've riches and you've lands,
But all those pretty ladies you must put them to one side,
For I'm the little gypsy girl that is to be your bride.

Now once I was a gypsy girl but now a squire's bride,
I've got servants for to wait on me and in me carriage ride,
The bells they rung so merrily and sweet the music did play,
And a jolly time we had upon the gypsy's wedding day.

The Beggarman

Words & Music: trad., arr. Jake Walton

This is a collated version of the „Gaberlunie Man" which is listed in the Child
Ballads as No. 279. The song has been collected from many Scottish singers
in much the same form and tells a romantic story with a happy ending where
a beggar turns out to be a rich Lord or King in disguise. I believe one Scottish
king did have the habit of dressing up disguised as a beggar and travelling the
countryside but I feel the story owes more to wishful thinking than reality! Part
of the charm of the song for me lies in the almost film-like imagery of the
storytelling, which appeals to adults and children alike. I found that an open
guitar tuning of C (cgcgcd) suits the song's melody.

Es handelt es sich hier um eine abgewandelte Fassung des Liedes „Gaberlunie Man", welches unter der Nummer 279 in den Cild Balladen verzeichnet ist. In der gleichen Fassung ist es von zahlreichen schottischen Sängern übernommen worden und erzählt die romantische und glücklich ausgehende Geschichte, in der sich ein Bettler als verkleideter Edelmann oder König entpuppt. Ich vermute, sie erzählt, ein schottischer König hätte die Angewohnheit gehabt, als Bettler kostümiert durchs Land zu ziehen. Aber ich gehe mal davon aus, daß diese Geschichte wohl mehr Wunsch als Wirklichkeit war. Für mich macht die filmreife Handlung des Liedes seinen besonderen Zauber aus, der Erwachsene wie Kinder gleichermaßen anspricht. Eine offene Gitarrenstimmung des C (cgcgcd) passt meines Erachtens gut zur Melodie.

Oh a beggarman came o'er the lea
With many good e'ens and good days to me.
Saying good wife for your charity
Will you lodge a beggarman.

Chorus:
Lassie to my tow row ray,
Lassie to my tow row ray.

The night was cold, the carl was wet,
And down upon the hearth he sat,
The farmers daughter he took by the hand,
And laughed as he sang.

(Chorus)

Oh if I were black as I am white
As the snow, that lies on yonder dyke
I'd dress myself some beggar like
And with you I'd go.

(Chorus)

Oh lassie, lassie you're far too young,
And you 'aint the cant of the begging tongue,
No you 'aint the cant of the begging tongue,
And with me you cannot go.

(Chorus)

I'll bend my back, I'll crook my knee,
I'll put a black patch on my eye.
And for a beggar they'll take me,
We shall be merry and sing.

(Chorus)

Oh then these two they made a plot
To rise an hour before the cock,
So gently as she slipped the lock
And through the fields they ran.

(Chorus)

Oh well early next morning the old wife arose,
And to her daughters bed she goes
The bed was bare, the sheets were cold,
She's away with the beggarman.

(Chorus)

Some looked on horeback and some of foot,
The wife was mad half out her wits,
She cursed, she swore, she rued the day,
Ere she lodged the beggarman.

(Chorus)

The years had passed some two or three,
The same old man came o'er the lea,
Saying good wife for your charity
Will you lodge a beggarman.

(Chorus)

A beggar, a beggar I'll ne'er lodge again,
For I had a daughter but only one,
And with a beggarman she's gone,
And I know not whence nor where.

(Chorus)

Oh well yonder she's coming to your bower
In silk and satins and many's the flower,
She's held up her hands, she's blest the hour,
Ere she saw the beggarman.

(Chorus)

Sunlight And Shade

Words & Music: Jake Walton

The mechanisation of farms and agriculture and the widespread arrival of the motor car to Britain by the 1950's led to the rapid decline in the use of the horse on the farms and roads up and down the country. It also spelt the end of the traditional way of life for the Romany people, who up until that time lived and travelled in horse drawn wagons. This song was written about those days of „Wagon-time" and is dedicated to a true Romany called Ceth, a musician and free spirit, who travelled in the Midlands of England.

Die Mechanisierung auf den Bauernhöfen und in der Landwirtschaft sowie die flächendeckende Motorisierung führte in den 1950er Jahren überall zu einem raschen Rückgang des Einsatzes von Pferden bei Ackerbau und Transportwesen. Sie hatte auch ein Ende der traditionellen Lebensweisen der Roma zur Folge, die bis dahin in und mit ihren Pferdewagen lebten und übers Land zogen. Dieses Lied beschreibt jene „Wagen-Zeit" und ist einem Roma namens Ceth gewidmet; ein Musiker und Freigeist, der in Mittelengland unterwegs gewesen ist.

Intro D

D

You came   by   a   wood-land

Em

A5

stream   whi-stled your   song   so _____ shrill, __   in   the

D

G

A7

green glades, __   your horses __ drank   their __ fill __   g - y psy

Ref. D

A5

D

tell   me, what you've   seen,   in   the   sun-light __ and

A5

G   D   A5

Guitar

sh-ade __   in   the sun-light _____ and the sh-ade.

D

A5

D

Ending

Em

A5

In   the   sun - light _____   of   a   sum-mer's

D

Em

dawn _____   by   fire light _____

A5

D

when   shad-ows   fall _____   in   the

Em

A5

sun - light _____   of   a   sum-mer's

28

Guit. tuning: DADGAD

You came by a woodland stream,
And you whistled your song so shrill,
In the green glades,
Your horses drank their fill.

Chorus:
And Gipsy tell me, what you've seen,
In the sunlight and the shade,
Between the sunlight and the shade.

By the hedgerow on a summers dawn,
There's a light in the eastern sky,
Your dogs bark,
Your waggon rolls on by.
(Chorus)

Your coal black eyes, your carefree ways,
Felt the change in the autumn breeze,
You knew the wild song,
Of the wind tossed trees.

(Chorus)

By the open fire on a winters eve,
The valley lies so still,
The first owls call,
There's a moon upon the hill.

(Chorus)

29

You came from a far distant land,
You travelled the roads so free,
And your Romany ways,
Are shrouded deep in mystery.

(Chorus)

You came by a woodland stream,
And you whistled your song so shrill,
In the green glades,
Your horses drank their fill.

(Chorus)

Ending

In the Sunlight of a Summer's dawn,
By fivelight when shadows fall.
In the Sunlight of a Summer's dawn.

The Trees They Do Grow High

Words: trad.
Music: trad., arr. Jake Walton

Sometimes known as „Still Growing" or the „Bonny Boy" this widespread ballad has been found in England, Scotland and Ireland. Child marriages in aristocratic families were common and it has been suggested that the ballad was originally Scottish and that the boy was Lord Creighton who married the daughter of his guardian Sir Robert Innes in 1631. He died in 1634. I found that using an open D tuning on the guitar and focusing on chords from the relative minor seemed to compliment the songs sad story and give it a Celtic harp-like sound.

Diese gängige Ballade ist in England, Schottland und Ireland auch als „Still Growing" oder „The Bonny Boy" bekannt. In aristokratischen Familien war Kinderheirat lange allgemein üblich. Angeblich soll die Ballade schottischen Ursprungs sein und der Junge ein gewisser Lord Creighton, der 1631 die Tochter seines Vormund Sir Robert Creighton heiratete. Er starb im Jahre 1634. Ich denke, eine Beschränkung auf eine offene D Stimmung und Moll-Akkorde passt gut zur traurigen Geschichte des Liedes und verleihen ihm die Klangfarbe der keltischen Harfe.

Guit. tuning: DADF#AD

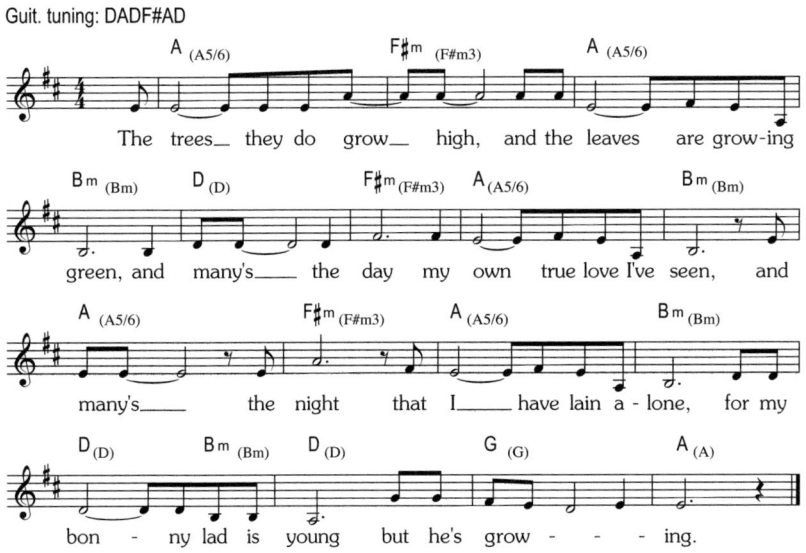

31

The trees they do grow high, and the leaves are growing green,
And many's the day my own true love I've seen,
And many's the night that I have lain alone,
For my bonny lad is young but he's growing.

Oh father, dear father, you've done to me much wrong,
You've married me to a boy who is too young,
He is but fourteen and I am twenty-one,
Oh the bonny lad is young but he's growing.

Oh daughter, dear daughter, I've done to you no wrong,
I've married you to a wealthy Lord's son,
A lady he'll make you, aye when you'll be made
For the bonny lad is young but he's growing.

We'll send your love to college for a year or two,
And in that time perhaps he'll do for you,
And all around his waist we'll tie a ribbon blue,
To let the ladies know that he's married.

At the age of fourteen he was a married man,
At the age of sixteen the father to a son,
And at the age of eighteen the grass was over him,
For death had put an end to his growing.

Tristan's Song

Words: Jake Walton
Music: Jake Walton

The story of Tristan and Isolde, an Arthurian legend, is one of the most popular love stories of Western Europe. Lyonesse is the lost land to the west of Cornwall, which has also been linked to Atlantis. In olden times when a couple were to be married they would drink a special love potion. Tristan and Isolde mistakenly drank of such a potion and fell in love, even though Isolde was to be married to King Mark.

Die Erzählung von Tristan und Isolde aus der Arthus-Sage ist eine der populärsten Liebesgeschichten Westeuropas. Lyonesse gilt als das versunkene Land im Westen Cornwalls, das auch mit Atlantis in Verbindung gebracht worden ist. In alten Zeiten nahmen Brautpare einen besonderen Liebestrank zu sich. Tristan und Isolde kosteten versehentlich davon und verliebten sich darauf ineinander, obwohl Isolde dem König Mark zur Frau versprochen war.

For my uncle Mark of Cornwall I journeyd o'er the sea,
To Ireland to gain the favour of the King and company,
For the fair daughter Isolde I chanced to risk my own life,
For it was King Mark's wish for her to be his bride.

Disguised as a harper I came to the court,
I fought for the King his favour I bought,
I was granted my wish for Isolde's hand in marriage ot King Mark,
And with a love philtre from the Queen we did embark.

But as we journeyed homeward on the long sea one day,
We drank of the magic wine from the cask where it lay,
And our hearts became tied through the years from that day to this,
Aven though she could wed the King of Lyonesse.

Oh my name it is Tristan I come from the west,
I've served my King and the land of Lyonesse,
But the pain that I bear is far keener than the sword to endure,
For Isolde my love the time can't cure.

Standing Stones

Words: Jake Walton
Music: trad., arr. Jake Walton

I have visited many stone circles in Ireland, Scotland and Cornwall. They are all situated in beautiful countryside and hold for me a special magic. These religious megaliths predate the arrival of the Celts and possibly date back to 2000 B.C. I set these words to a traditional tune from the Orkney Islands having been inspired by the stone circle near St. Buryan in Cornwall called „The Merry Maidens". Close by are two solitary stones known as the „Pipers" Legend has it that the maidens and pipers were found dancing and playing music on a Sunday and were turned to stone as punishment! One of the first folk clubs I played in took its name from these stones and was called „The Pipers Folk Club". The singer Brenda Wootton ran it along with John the Fish.

Ich habe mir in Irland, Schottland und Cornwall eine Menge Steinkreise angesehen. Sie liegen alle in herrlichen Landschaften und bergen meines Erachtens einen besonderen Zauber. Solche religiösen Magelithen datieren wahrscheinlich vor der Ankunft der Kelten um 2000 vor unserer Zeitrechnung. Diese Verse habe ich mit einer überlieferten Melodie der Orkney-Inseln verbunden. Inspiriert durch den Steinkreis in der Nähe von St. Buryan in Cornwall, der „The Merry Maidens" genannt wird. Dicht daneben stehen zwei einzelne Steine, bekannt als „The Pipers". Der Legende nach sollen Mädchen und Piper an einem Sonntag bei Spiel und Tanz gesehen und zur Strafe in Steine verwandelt worden sein. Einer der ersten Folkclubs, in denen ich aufgetreten bin, war nach diesen Steinen als „The Piper's Folk Club" benannt. Er wurde von den Sängern Brenda Wootton und John the Fish geführt.

Far unto the western lands, down the winding road,
'tis there you'll find upon the hill, the circle of standing stones and ponder on the purpose, of hands in days of old, did hew the rock and mark the ground, for the circle of standing stones.

Guit. tuning: DADGAD
Capo 2nd fret
Play ( ) chords

Far unto the western lands, down the winding road,
'Tis there you'll find upon the hill, the circle of standing stones,
And ponder on the purpose, of hands in days of old,
Did hew the rock and mark the ground, for the circle of standing stones.

Shadows in the cloudy sky, their shape before me rose,
Silence filled the air around, the circle of standing stones,
Yet as I stood a-watching, the evening to it's close,
The wind it whistled this song around, the circle of standing stones.

It told of the power, which through the land could pass,
To cure the sick and heal the wound, or join two lover's hearts,
As night fell soft around me, and stars began to show,
I felt the magical power within, the circle standing stones.

35

Echoes

Words: Walter de la Mare
Music: Jake Walton

Walter De La Mare (1873 – 1956) was born in Kent, England. He wrote stories, plays and poems. Many of his poems are about nature. They have always held for me a special magic and sense of mystery. I set this one to music using the Dulcimer, which seemed to suit the poems' dreamlike feel.

Der Autor Walter de la Mare wurde 1873 im englischen Kent geboren und hat bis 1956 gelebt. Er verfasste Prosawerke, Theaterstücke und Gedichte. Viele seiner Gedichte handeln von der Natur. Für mich haben sie einen besonderen Zauber und eine mystische Ausstrahlung. Dieses Gedicht ist von mir für den Dulcimer vertont worden, der offenbar sehr gut zu seiner verträumten Stimmung passt.

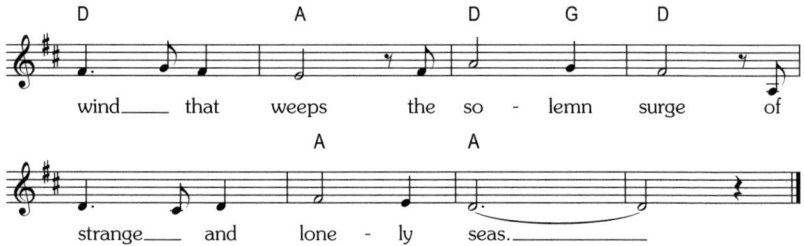

wind____ that weeps the so - lemn surge of
strange____ and lone - ly seas._____

The sea laments the live long day fringing its waste with sand,
Cries back the wind from the wisp'ring shore no words can I understand.

Yet echoes my heart a voice as far as near as these,
The wind that weeps the solemn surge of strange and lonely seas.

The Wheel of Fortune

Words: trad.
Music: trad., arr. Jez Lowe

I first met the singer Jez Lowe at the Pontardawe Celtic Festival in 1980. It was soon after this that we formed a part time duo and this song was in our early repertoire. It comes from the North East of England, Jez's homeland and was first printed as a broadside ballad by Hoggetts of Durham. It is now more of a lyric with few narrative details, but it contains several commonplace folk lines and phrases and it is Jez Lowe and Jed Foley who are responsible for this fine version.

Dem Sänger Jez Lowe bin ich zum ersten Mal 1990 auf dem Pontardare Celtic Festival begegnet. Kurz darauf kooperierten wir eine zeitlang als Duo und dieses Lied gehörte zu unserem frühen Repertoire. Es stammt aus Jez Heimat im Nordosten Englands und war erstmals als Broadside-Ballade von Hoggetts aus Durham gedruckt worden. Mittlerweile ist es eher lyrisch mit ein paar erzählerischen Details, es trägt aber auch einige folkloristische Züge. Diese wunderbare Fassung geht auf Jez Lowe und Jed Foley zurück.

It's after morn there comes an evening,
After evening another day,
And after false love comes annother,
It's hard to keep them who will away.

Chorus:
So turn you around you wheel of fortune,
Turn you around and smile on me,
Loving words are quite uncertain,
Sad experience teaches me.

If I had known before I courted,
Love was oh so ill to win,
I'd have locked my heart in a box of golden,
And tied it with a silver pin.

(Chorus)

Do you recall our days of courting,
With your sweet head laid on my breast,
You could make me believe with a touch of your hand,
The morning sun rose in the west.

(Chorus)

Winter brings an end to summer,
Green leaves fall from every tree,
Time will bring an end to all things,
Love will bring an end to me.

(Chorus)

The Curragh Of Kildare

Words & Music: trad., arr. Jake Walton

This was one of the songs which inspired me and I am sure many others to be drawn into Irish folk song and music. I first heard it sung by the Furey Brothers and later by Bert Jansch who did a beautiful arrangement of it on his album „A Rare Conundrum". It is thought that the Curragh of Kildare may refer to a racecourse in Ireland of the same name.

Dies war eines jener Lieder, die mich – und ich bin sicher, auch viele andere – dem irischen Folksong und der irischen Musik nahe gebracht haben. Erstmals hörte ich es von den Furey-Brüdern, später von Bert Jansch, der eine ausgezeichnete Bearbeitung für sein Album „A Rare Conundrum" aufgenommen hat. Man nimmt an, dass sich der Titel auf eine irische Pferderennbahn gleichen Namens bezieht.

The win-ter it is past and the sum-mers come at last,
the small birds__ are sing - ing in the trees, their
lit - tle hearts are glad,__ ah but mine is ve - ry sad for my
own true love's far__ a - way from me. And it's
straight I will re - pair to the Cur - ragh__ of__ Kil - dare,
for it's there I'll find tid - ings__ of__ my dear.

Capo 5th Fret
Play ( ) Chords

The winter it is passed and the summers come at last
The small birds are singing in the trees
Their little hearts are glad
Ah but mine is very sad
For my own true love's far away from me.

Chorus:
And it's straight I will repair
To the curragh of Kildare
For it's there I'll find tidings of my dear.

The rose upon the briar and the water's running clear
Charms the heart of the linnet and the bee
Their little lives are blest

Ah but mine can find no rest
For my own true love's far away from me.

(Chorus)

A livery I'll wear and I'll tie back my hair
In velvet so green I will appear
And this I'll undertake
For my own true love's sake
For she lives in the curragh of kildare.

(Chorus)

I'll wear a cap of black with some frills around my neck
Golden rings on my fingers I will wear
And it's straight I will repair
To the curragh of kildare
For it's there I'll find tidings of my dear.

(Chorus)

Oh you who are in love and cannot it deny
I pity the pain you do endure
For experience lets me know
That your hearts are full of woe
And a woe that no mortal man can cure.

(Chorus)

The West Wind

Words: John Masefield
Music: Jake Walton

Cornwall is the south-westernmost county of the British Isles and has been my home now for a long time. My musical life began there in the 1960's when I met many of the musicians who first inspired me and who later went on to become collaborators and friends. This moving poem of homecoming by John Masefield always reminds me of those early days and is why „The white road westward" will always carry special memories.

Cornwall ist der südwestlichste Bezirk der Britischen Inseln und seit langem meine Heimat. Dort begann in den 1960ern mein musikalisches Leben, als ich vielen Musikern begegnete, die mich als erste inspirierten und später zu Mitstreitern und Freunden wurden. Das bewegende Gedicht von John Masefield über Heimkehr erinnert mich stets an jene Jugendzeit und warum mich „The white road westward" stets mit besonderen Erinnerungen verbindet.

44

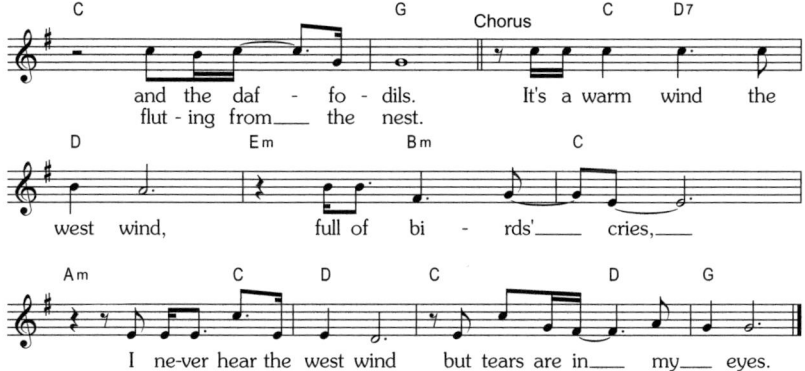

and the daf - fo - dils. It's a warm wind the
flut - ing from____ the nest.
west wind, full of bi - rds'____ cries,____
I ne-ver hear the west wind but tears are in____ my____ eyes.

Bridge: C6 | C6 | A7 | D7 | D7

It's a warm wind the west wind, full of birds' cries,
I never hear the west wind but tears are in my eyes,
It comes from the west land, those old brown hills,
And April's in the west wind and the daffodils.

It's a fine land the west land, for hearts as tired as mine,
The apple orchards blossom there and the air's like wine,
There's cool green grass there, where men may lay at rest,
And the thrushes are in song there, fluting from the nest.

Chorus:
It's a warm wind the west wind, full of birds' cries,
I never hear the west wind but tears are in my eyes.

Come home now brother for you've been long away,
It's April and it's blossom time and white is the may,
And bright is the sun and warm is the rain,
Will you come home brother, home to us again?

(Chorus)

The white road westward is the road that I must tread,
To the cool grass, the green grass and rest for heart and head,
To the violets and the warm hearts and the thrushes song,
In the fine land, the west land where I belong.

(Chorus)

45

Song Of Parting

Words: Jake Walton.
Music: Trad. / Jake Walton

This is a song of lost love. The melody is from Galicia in Spain and is very old. I know little of its history but I have always enjoyed playing it on the Hurdy-Gurdy and I recorded it on my LP „Sunlight and Shade" with the help of Eric Liorzou (guitar) and Stephen Cooney (fretless bass) in the early 1980's.

I remember one cold January night playing in a club in Dublin where an enthusiastic member of the audience gave me a teddy bear as a token of thanks after the gig. This caused great amusement to my friends, Joe and Antoinette McKenna, with whom I was staying at the time! Nevertheless the next evening in the local pub with my friends I came up with the idea and most of the words for this song, so I would like to belatedly thank that person (and the bear) for the inspiration they gave me!

Ein Lied über Liebesverlust. Die Melodie stammt aus dem spanischen Galizien und ist sehr alt. Über ihre Geschichte weiß ich nur wenig, aber ich trage sie gern mit der Drehleier vor und habe das Lied mit Hilfe von Eric Liorzou (Gitarre) und Stephen Cooney (Fretless Bass) in den frühen 1980ern für meine LP „Sunlight And Shade" aufgenommen.

Ich erinnere mich an eine kalte Januar-Nacht, als ich in einem Dubliner Club spielte und ein Fan aus dem Publikum mir nach dem Auftritt als Zeichen seiner Wertschätzung einen Teddybär zum Geschenk machte. Was meine Freunde Joe und Antoinette McKenna, bei denen ich damals wohnte, köstlich amüsiert hat. Als ich den nächsten Abend mit meinen Freunden in ihrem Stammpub verbrachte, kamen mir die Verse für dieses Lied in den Sinn und so möchte ich mich nachträglich bei den Mensch (und dem Bär) für die Inspiration bedanken.

Aye aye an an nay na na, aye
aye an an nay na na.

You say at home you're there alone,
That I know it cannot be,
There's one when day is through,
At our door he calls for you.

Chorus:
Aye aye an an nay na na,
Aye aye an an nay na na.

In pale skies swallows fly,
I've watched them dive to the river,
But now they're gone it seems,
Leaving just a few sad dreams.

(Chorus)

Ribbons tied in your hair,
Memories haunt where ere I go,
Strange how we never knew,
That our days should be so few.

(Chorus)

Joys they stand as shifting sand,
And our first love has proved untrue,
Strange how I could not see,
That soon we'd parted be.

(Chorus)

You say at home you're there alone,
That I know it cannot be,
Strange how I could not see,
That you'd unfaithful be.

(Chorus)

The Quiet Lands Of Erin

Words: trad.
Music: trad., arr. Jake Walton

I heard a story that this song was written by a man from Co. Antrim in Ireland. He was about to emigrate but on boarding his ship was so overcome with regret to be leaving his homeland that he changed his mind and came ashore again before the boat set sail. He then went back home and wrote this song, spending the rest of his days happily, „In the Quiet lands above the sea". I do not know if the story is true but it is a lovely song. I first heard it performed by Finbar and Eddie Fury in the late 1960's and it has remained a favourite of mine ever since.

Dem Vernehmen nach soll dieses Lied von einem Mann aus dem County Antrim in Irland stammen. Er war im Begriff auszuwandern, doch beim Einschiffen kamen ihm Bedenken, seine Heimat zu verlassen und er ging von Bord noch bevor das Schiff in See stach. Wieder daheim, schrieb er dieses Lied und ward glücklich bis ans Ende seiner Tage. Keine Ahnung, ob die Geschichte stimmt, aber es ist ein toller Song. Ich habe ihn in den späten 1960ern von Finbar und Eddie Furey gehört, seither zählt er zu meinen Favoriten.

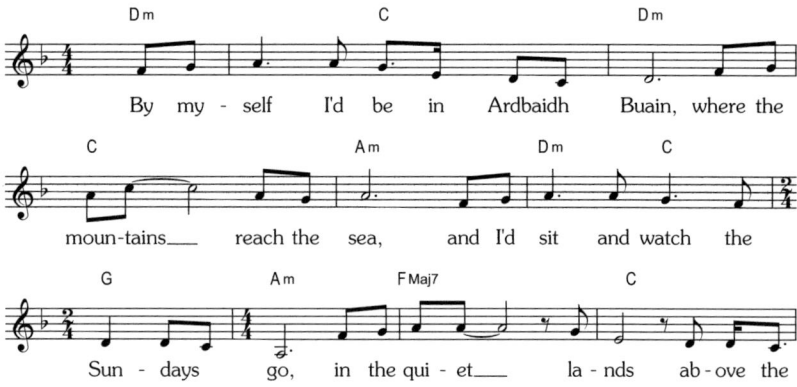

sea.   A - gus och   a Eire lig is   o,   Ei - re

Lon - dubh___   is___   o,   hear the   qui - et___

lands_____   of_____   E_____ rin. __

Guit. tuning: DADGBE

By myself I'd be in Arbaidh Buain
Where the mountains reach the sea
And I'd sit and watch the Sunday's go
In the quiet lands above the sea.

Chorus:
Agus och a Eire lig is o
Eire Londubh is o
Hear the quiet lands of Erin.

Oh my heart is weary all alone
And it sends a lonely cry
To the land that seems beyond dreams
While the lonely Sunday's pass me by.

(Chorus)

I'd rather back the twisted years
In the bitter hasted winds
If the God above would let me lie
In the quiet lands above the wind.

(Chorus)

The Valley Lay Smiling

Words & Music: trad., arr. Jake Walton

I learnt this Irish song from Pete Douglas and the melody comes from a tune called „Pretty Maid Milking a Cow" and was reputedly stolen from a fairy piper. It is considered unwise to play it seated near a „Rath" or fairy dwelling, for fear of displeasing the „Merry Gentry". I have rewritten it a little and changed the meaning. Legend has it that the old Irish bards sometimes would have a vision of Ireland as a beautiful woman. In the song the woman has been driven from her home so the story could be seen to be somewhat allegorical and refer to injustice or division in the world.

Dieses Lied hat mir Pete Douglas beigebracht. Angeblich wurde die Melodie einem Piper geklaut, der zu den Elfen gehörte. Deshalb sollte man es niemals in der Nähe von Orten spielen, an denen sich Elfen aufhalten um nicht ihren Unmut zu erregen. Ich habe es etwas überarbeitet und seine Aussage variiert. Es geht die Legende, dass die alten irischen Barden Irland manchmal als schöne Frau sahen. In dem Lied wurde die Frau aus ihrer Heimat vertrieben und so kann man die Geschichte auch als Allegorie für das Unrecht begreifen, in alle Welt verstreut zu werden.

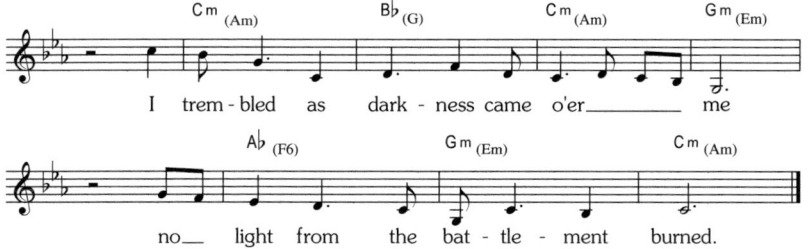

I trem - bled as dark - ness came o'er_____ me
no__ light from the bat - tle - ment burned.

Guit. tuning: DADGBE
Capo 3rd Fret
Play ( ) Chords

Oh the valley lay smiling before me
Where lately I'd left her behind
But I trembled as something came o'er me
That saddened the joy of my mind.
I looked for the lamp which she told me
Would shine when her pilgrim returned
I trembled as darkness came o'er me
No light from the battlement burned.

Oh I stood by her chamber so lonely
As if the loved tenant were dead
Oh would it were death and death only
Ah but no the young woman was fled.
And there hung the lute that could soften
My very worst pain into bliss
But the hand that played it so often
Was turned to another ones kiss.

And the valley lay smiling before me
Where lately I'd left her behind
But I trembled as something came o'er me
That saddened the joy of my mind.
I looked for the lamp which she told me
Would shine when her pilgrim returned
I trembled as darkness came o'er me
No light from the battlement burned.

All That's Past

Words: Walter de la Mare
Music: Jake Walton

This poem by Walter de la Mare (1873 –1956) could be seen as a lament for the passing of beauty, urging us to look on lovely things as if we may never see them again. However it seems also to remind that though the brook flows and passes, it still remains, like the rose. The rose is a Goddess symbol for the Celts and the poem for me is full of beautiful images of nature and our place in it.

Das Gedicht von Walter de la Mare (1873 – 1956) kann man als Klagelied auf die Vergänglichkeit von Schönheit verstehen, das uns mahnt, so auf die guten Dinge zu achten, als ob wir sie nie wieder zu Gesicht bekämen. Desgleichen erinnert es uns daran, daß der Bach gleich einer Rose immer bleibt und doch vorbei fließt. Für die Kelten war die Rose ein göttliches Symbol. Und für mich bergen diese Zeilen wunderbare Bilder der Natur und unserem Platz in ihr.

52

Very old are the woods;
And the buds that break
Out of the brier's boughs,
When March winds wake,
So old with their beauty are-
Oh, no man knows
Through what wild centuries
Roves back the rose.

Very old are the brooks;
And the rills that rise
Where snow sleeps cold beneath
The azure skies
Sing such a history
Of come and gone,
Their every drop is as wise
As Solomon.

Very old are we men;
Our dreams are tales
Told in dim Eden
By Eve's nightingales;
We wake and whisper awhile,
But, the day gone by,
Silence and sleep like fields
Of amaranth lie.

Very old are the woods;
And the buds that break
Out of the brier's boughs,
When March winds wake,
So old with their beauty are-
Oh, no man knows
Through what wild centuries
Roves back the rose.

Patrick's Song

Words: Jake Walton
Music: Patrick Ewen

This song was originally learned from the Breton group Bleizi Ruz and was sung by their part time vocalist Patrik Ewen. The band's original version can be heard on the album „Bleizi Ruz En Concert", where it is called „Voyaget M'Eus E Bro Vreiz". It proved popular with audiences in the U.S.A. when Jez Lowe and I toured there in the 1980's. I remember that the sight of two English guys alighting from an ancient Cadillac called Alexander, (on loan from our agent Amy Fonoroff) which had a „Dump Reagan" sticker on the bumper also caused a fair amount of interest at the time! I set my own words to the melody, which are somewhat autobiographical and the second verse is also a thank you to Bert Jansch and Donovan, whose music and songs have meant so much to me over the years.

Ursprünglich stammt dieses Lied von der bretonischen Gruppe Bleizi Ruz und wurde von ihrem zeitweisen Sänger Patrick Ewen gesungen. Die Originalfassung findet sich auf dem Album „Bleizi Ruz En Concert", wo es den Titel „Voyaget M'Eus E Bro Vreiz" trägt. Es erfreute sich beim Publikum in den USA großer Beliebtheit, als ich dort in den 1980ern mit Jez Lowe auf Tournee war. Ich erinnere mich, dass damals der Anblick von zwei englischen Burschen, die aus einem alten Cadillac mit Namen Alexander (ausgeliehen von unserem Agentin Amy Fonoroff) stiegen, an dessen Stoßstange ein „Dump Reagan!" Sticker klebte, eine Menge Aufmerksamkeit erregt hat. Zu der Melodie habe ich meine eigenen Verse verfasst, die ein paar autobiographische Züge tragen. Und die zweite Strophe ist ein Dank an Bert Jansch und Donovan, deren Musik und Lieder mir in all den Jahren viel bedeutet haben.

Intro G

G

I was bo - rn____ a son of the wan - der - ing___ race, and

may I ne-ver tire of my gyp - s - ying ways, like a

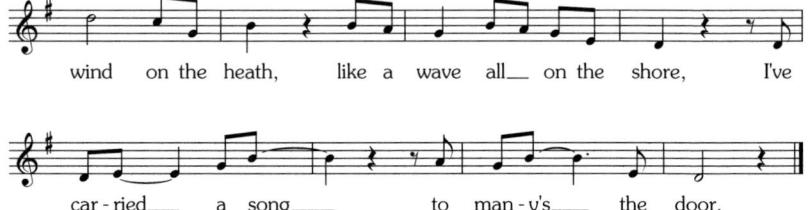

wind on the heath, like a wave all__ on the shore, I've

car - ried__ a song__ to man - y's__ the door.

I was born a son of the wandering race,
And may I never tire of my gypsying ways,
Like a wind on the heath, like a wave all on the shore,
I've carried a song to many's the door.

And I followed the rhyme that the minstrel boy sang,
Stood on the beach where the long breezes ran,
It was then I could tell that the time was come,
To catch dreams from the clouds and try for the sun.

And I once loved a girl from a far and foreign land,
But the future and fate was not ours to command,
Still her memory I'll hold though it grieves my heart sore,
That her dark dancing eyes I may ne'er see no more.

I'll go back to the life that I love so well,
With a song in my heart and a story to tell,
When misfortune falls and the road turns so slow,
Let the lantern shine bright to guide where'ere I go.

Black Sarah

Wors & Music: Lorraine A. Lee-Hammond

This song was written by Lorraine Lee Hammond the Dulcimer player from Boston U.S.A. Legend has it that in A.D. 42 two of the Biblical sisters of the Virgin Mary landed at Saintes Maries de la Mer in the South of France in a small boat in which they had drifted from the Holy Land. Travelling with them was an Egyptian serving girl called Sarah. Sarah-la-Kali or Black Sarah became the patron saint of the Romany Gypsies and is honoured by them at Saintes Maries each year in a festival. Lorraine wrote the song after reading the book „Gypsies, Wanderers of the World" which I had asked her to find for me in America. The book retraces the travels of the Romany people who left north India about 1000 years ago and migrated west, arriving in England in the early 16 th century. After I had learnt of the story of Black Sarah, I found it interesting that many Black Madonnas have been rediscovered in Europe in recent years and current interest in them may relate to a search for the lost feminine earth-wisdom.

Dieses Lied hat die Dulcimer-Spielerin Lorraine Lee Hammond aus Boston / USA geschrieben. Der Legende nach landeten Anno 42 n. Chr. die Schwestern der Jungfrau Maria in einem kleinen Boot beim heutigen Saintes Maries de la Mer an der südfranzöischen Mittelmeerküste, das sie aus dem heiligen Land hierher gebracht hatte. Sie reisten in Begleitung einer ägyptischen Dienerin namens Sarah. Sarah-la-Kali oder die schwarze Sarah wurde zur Schutzpatronin der Romani und wird von ihnen jedes Jahr mit einem Fest geehrt. Lorraine verfasste das Lied nach der Lektüre des Buches „Gypsies – Wanderers of the World", das sie für mich in Amerika besorgen sollte. Das Buch verfolgt die Wanderungen der Romani zurück, die vor etwa 11.000 Jahren Indien in Richtung Westen verließen und im frühen 16. Jahrhundert England erreichten. Als ich von der Geschichte der schwarzen Sarah erfahren hatte, fiel mir auf, dass in der jüngeren Vergangenheit in Europa viele schwarze Madonnen wiederentdeckt worden sind und das derzeitige Interesse mit der Suche nach dem vergessenen weiblichen Weltwissen zusammen hängt.

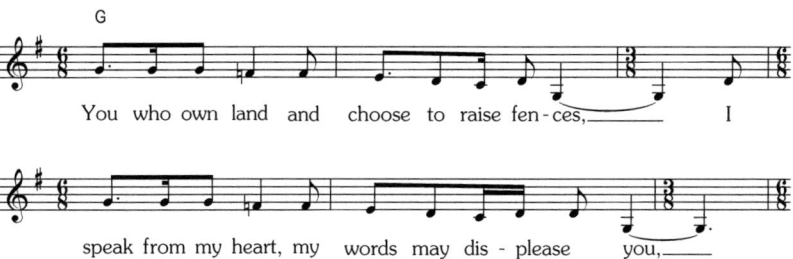

You who own land and choose to raise fen-ces,⸻ I speak from my heart, my words may dis-please you,⸻

Instrumental

Black Sa - rah pro - tect me.

The Good God in heaven, he meant all his peo - ple,

to live as they choose with-out har-ming each o - ther.

You are no lon - ger my bro - ther,— for you have

stopped me and my fami - ly from drink - ing of God's own clear

streams and graz - ing our hor - ses.

You who own land and choose to raise fences,
I speak from my heart, my words may displease you,
Black Sarah protect me.

The Good God in heaven, he meant all his people,
To live as they chose without harming each other.
You are no longer my brother, for you have stopped me and my family
From drinking of God's own clear streams and grazing our horses.

I was born on the road, raised in field and in forest,
Now I live in a broken down caravan park,
Black Sarah console me.

I dream of the past, with the seasons we circled,
How can we call only one place our home?
You would make our lives bleak as your own.

You surround us with laws,
And with government forms.
Try to teach our children you ways, but their hearts will choose freedom.

I try to forget nightmares,
I read in your palms, I take only your money.
Black Sarah forgive me.

Lead me, I pray as you led the two Mary's,
With love and strength led them safe to land.
Help me understand that although I am a poor woman,
The eyes of my children dance with my love.
Their laughter delights me.

September Morning

Words & Music: Jake Walton

I wrote this song many years ago in Cornwall after a time spent away travelling. It has a meditative feel about it and I tried to link together the themes of solitude and peace of mind on my return.

Dieses Lied habe ich vor vielen Jahren nach einer langen Abwesenheit in Cornwall geschrieben. Es hat eine nachdenkliche Grundstimmung und versucht, die Gefühle von Einsamkeit und Seelenfrieden meiner Rückkehr miteinander zu verknüpfen.

Guit. tuning: DGDGBD

I sat down by the river
To watch the water go by,
My life was much quieter in those days,
Just the wind and the stars in the sky.

Over the green seas, I wandered
To the grey grey mountains so cold,
To the sound of the seas on the beaches
And the squeak of the sand beneath my toes.

People try to make it so many ways,
And use their time in vain,
Treading a path to no avail,
Trying to laugh at the rain.

Yet on that misty september morning,
Though the sky seemed far from blue,
As I watched the autumn leaves falling,
The sun came through.

The Reign Of The Fair Maid

Words & Music: Jake Walton

The basis of this song is from an old English carol, although its roots go back
to pre-Christian Celtic myth. The Fair Maid was sometimes known as Bridghe,
a multifaceted goddess of knowledge, life and the mother of poets. It is she
who turns the wheel of the year. In the spring she is a maiden, in the summer
a mother and in autumn she becomes a wise woman before being reborn the
following year.

Grundlage dieses Liedes ist ein alter englischer Choral, seine Ursprünge gehen allerdings auf vorchristliche keltische Mythen zurück. The Fair Maid war
manchmal als Bridghe geläufig, eine vielgesichtige Göttin der Weisheit, des
Lebens und Mutter der Poesie. Sie ist es, die das Jahresrad dreht. Im Frühjahr
Mädchen, im Sommer Mutter und im Herbst eine weise Frau, bevor sie im folgenden Jahr wiedergeboren wird.

61

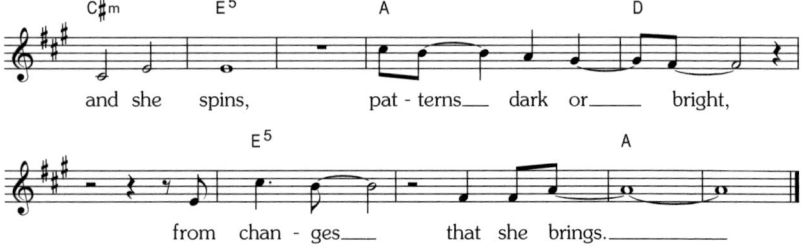

and she spins, pat - terns___ dark or___ bright,

from chan - ges___ that she brings._____

Guit. tuning: EADEAE

The reign of the Fair Maid, with gold on her chin,
She opens the east door, to let the New Year in.
Like a wheel she turns winter into spring,
And life to the green bough is the gift that she brings.

Chorus:
Through the days of our life, she weaves and she spins,
Patterns dark or bright, from changes that she brings.

The reign of the Fair Maid with gold on her toe,
She opens the west door, to let the old year go.
The long days of summer, soon they grow old,
As she turns to the autumn, and the cold winds that blow.

(Chorus)

The reign of the Fair Maid, with gold on her chin,
She opens the east door, to let a new year in.
Time and the season, she holds in her sway,
And the parts we take are cast in her play.

(Chorus)

Trees

Words: Jake Walton
Music: Jake Walton / Eric Liorzou

I remember how sad it was when Dutch elm disease came to the U.K. in the 1970's and this song was inspired by an old folk story, that I heard at the time, which told of how the oak tree grew in the shelter of the Elm tree and if the Elm died then the Oak would also perish. In fact now that the English Elm has all but vanished the oak is also threatened. The first part of the melody of the song is based on an old Breton dance tune, which I learnt from Eric Liorzou.

Ich erinnere mich noch, wie schlimm es war, als sich in den 1970er Jahren im Vereinigten Königreich die holländische Ulmenkrankheit ausbreitete. Dieses Lied ist durch eine alte Volkssage inspiriert, die ich damals kennengelernt habe. Sie erzählt davon, wie eine Eiche im Schutz einer Ulme wuchs und zugrunde gehen müßte, falls die Ulme sterben sollte. Da es mittlerweile kaum noch englische Ulmen gibt, ist nun auch die Eiche bedroht. Der erste Teil des Liedes basiert auf einer alten bretonischen Tanzmelodie, die mir Eric Liorzou beigebracht hat.

Guit. tuning: DADGAD. Capo 2nd Fret. Play ( ) Cords

sigh, for the trees that once hung lay - den,__
lay__ stripped 'neath the sum-mer's sk - y____

I returned one summer's day,
Where childhood years were spent in play,
Down the paths that oft I'd strayed,
Deep into the forest,deep into the forest,
But time cast its season and I cast a sigh,
For the trees that once hung laden,
lay stripped 'neath the summer's sky.

Down through the years the tall tree,
The wayside briar, ash and beech,
The willow by the running stream were here long before me,
They were here long before me,
And the trees give the shelter,
And the shade from the summer sun
And the fireside bright at evening,
When the winter night draws in.

Poets told of the woodland scene,
Silent grace of ancient trees,
Makers of the air we breathe,
Guardians of life, the guardians of life,
For the tree is the symbol, of the life force which flows
Is drawn ever upwards as in truth the spirit grows.

The oak and elm together grow,
Standing close in friendship's hold,
Leaves of deepest green unfold,
Lords of the forest, lords of the forest,
But the elm lies a-dying,
And the oak gives a sigh
To a long, long and a trusty friend,
To an old friend a sigh.

(The Lake Isle Of) Innisfree

Words: William Butler Yeats
Music: Jake Walton

This poem by the Irish poet William Butler Yeats (1865 – 1939) is one of his most famous. It is thought that he found the inspiration for it when walking down the Strand in London and saw raindrops on a shop window. This brought back childhood memories of his beloved County Sligo and the Isle of Innisfree. The love of solitude and nature is a very Celtic trait, beautifully expressed here.

Dieses Gedicht des irischen Dichters William Buttler Yeats (1865 – 1939) ist eines seiner berühmtesten Werke. Es heißt, er sei dazu bei einem Spaziergang auf The Strand (in London zwischen Trafalgar Square und Fleet Street) inspiriert worden, als er Regentropfen an einem Schaufenster perlen sah, welche bei ihm Kindheitserinnerungen an seine geliebte Heimat County Sligo auslösten. Die Wertschätzung von Einsamkeit und Natur ist ein typisch „keltischer" Charakterzug, der hier wunderbar zum Ausdruck gebracht wird.

Guit. tuning: DADGBE Capo 2nd Fret. Play ( ) Chords

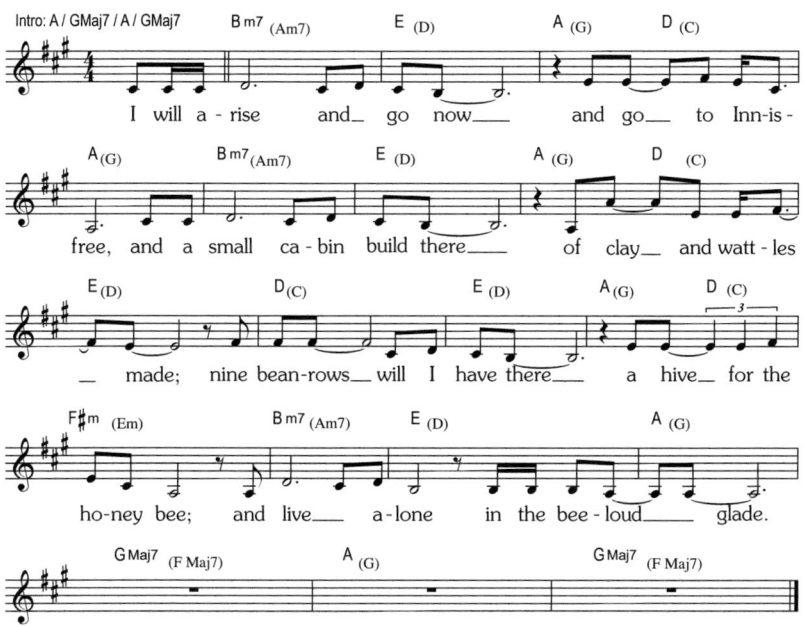

I will arise and go now and go to Innisfree,
And a small cabin build there of clay and wattles made;
Nine bean rows will I have there a hive for the honey bee;
And live alone in the bee-loud glade.

And I shall have some peace there, for peace comes dropping slow,
Dropping from the veils of the morning to where the cricket sings;
There midnight's all a glimmer, and noon a purple glow,
And evening full of the linnet's wings.

I will arise and go now, for always night and day
I hear lake water lapping with low sounds by the shore;
While I stand on the roadway, or on the pavements gray,
I hear it in the deep heart's core.

Gold And Silver

Words & Music: Jake Walton

I wrote this song specifically for a benefit tour for Friends Of The Earth in
1984. I remember at the time that people were very skeptical about concern
over the environment. One shop in my local town felt unable to publicize a gig
as they thought it might upset their customers; some people even crossed the
street to avoid me. Nowadays such issues are high on the political agenda and
attitudes have changed, although people still sometimes cross the street to
avoid me! Joking aside however it seems to me that the greatest challenge we
face today, is to learn, not only to live in harmony and peace with each other
but also with this incredibly beautiful planet that we inhabit, before it is too
late.

Den Song habe ich 1984 speziell für eine Tournee zur Unterstützung der
Friends Of The Earth geschrieben. Ich erinnere mich an Zeiten, in denen man
dem Umweltschutz mit großer Skepsis begegnete. Ein Laden in meinem Hei-
matort sah sich aus Furcht vor Verärgerung seiner Kunden außerstande, eines
meiner Konzertplakate auszuhängen, manche wechselten sogar die Straßenseite, um mir nicht zu begegnen. Heutzutage stehen Umweltthemen ganz oben
auf der Agenda und die Einstellungen haben sich gewandelt, auch wenn gele-
gentlich immer noch Leute die Straßenseite wechseln, um mir nicht über den
Weg zu laufen... Aber Spaß beiseite: zu lernen, in Harmonie und Frieden
untereinander und mit diesem unglaublich schönen Planeten zu leben, den wir
bedrohen, scheint zu den größten Herausforderungen zu gehören, mit denen
wir konfrontiert sind.

Guit. tuning: DADGBE Intro: 8 bars. Em D Em7 EM Em D Em7 EM

When poppies stood in golden corn,
Upon our backs the sun was warm,
Wild flowers decked the country lanes,
And summer came again,
But the wonder of nature's precious chain,
Soon lies broken and torn with the wind of change,

Refrain:
It's gone for our gold and our silver,
Gone for our gold and our silver.

By river bank kingfisher flies,
His royal blue before our eye,
Otter swims with silver glide,
The heron, he waits the tide
But fast our poison now it flows,
And the fish lie dead upon the stone,

(Refrain)

And to the north the salmon go,
Where wooded hills are capped with snow,
Jeweled lakes lace through the land,
Beyond the mountains stand,
But the rain that's borne from southern shores,
It brings death with each drop that softly falls,

(Refrain)

And when our children they do grow,
How will we teach them, how will they know
The beauty of our earth and sky,
When so much will vanish and die?
The memory like a dream from long ago,
To remind us of the love our maker showed,

(Refrain)

Over Seal Sands

Words & Music: Jez Lowe

A song by Jez Lowe, recorded as a bonus track on the „Two A Roue" CD. It was partly inspired by my own commitment to the environmental organisations such as Greenpeace and Friends of the Earth and fitted in with other songs like „Gold and Silver", also on the album. Seal Sands is a piece of wasteland at the mouth of the River Tees, which supports bird colonies and wildlife and attracts many visitors. Jez was living just on its doorstep when he wrote this song.

Ein Song von Jez Lowe, den wir als Bonustrack für die CD „Two A Roue" aufgenommen haben. Er war zu einem Gutteil durch mein Eintreten für Umweltorganisationen wie Greenpeace und Friends of the Earth inspiriert und

68

passt gut zu anderen Liedern wie „Gold and Silver", die sich ebenfalls auf dem Album befinden. Seal Sands ist ein Stück Ödland an der Mündung des Flusses Tees, welches Vogelkolonien und Wild beherbergt und viele Besucher anzieht. Jez lebte praktisch an dessen Haustür, als er diesen Song verfasste.

Guit. tuning: DADGAD Capo 3rd Fret. Play ( ) Chords

Where this dirty old river gives into the sea,
As long as forever, they've needed to be,
All the birds of the air, choose their time to be there,
Over Seal Sands, over Seal Sands.

People watch them come in weather, sunshine or rain,
And they all know their fine feathers and fancy names,
Well, a tern I wouldn't know, from a gull flying low,
Over Seal Sands, over Seal Sands.

And who knows the names of those clouds in the sky,
That come from the towers and chimneys so high,
Like all that work and high pay, they're all drifting away,
Over Seal Sands, over Seal Sands.

And the birds all go wading in sulphur and steam,
And peck out their days in a dry toxic dream,
But how much longer will wings beat with instinct and bring,
Them over Seal Sands, Over Seal Sands?

Beyond The Veil

Words: Jake Walton / Jez Lowe
Music: Eric Liorzou

This is a song about the mystic veil, which appears in some form or other in most cultures. In the Celtic lands, it is thought that the evening of All Hallows is the time that the veil between the two worlds is at its most transparent. The falling of the last leaves marks the coming of the darkness as the world on its axis leans away from the light and warmth of the sun traveling on its endless journey. This was the season, which often brought hardship and sorrow through the long winter months as people awaited the rebirth of the year.

Ein Lied über den geheimnisvollen Dunstschleier, der in der einen oder anderen Form in den meisten Kulturen vorkommt. In keltischen Regionen wird erzählt, dass er am Abend vor Allerheiligen am durchsichtigsten sei. Das Fallen der letzten Blätter kündet die bevorstehende Dunkelheit an, wenn sich die Erdachse auf ihrer endlosen Reise gegen das Licht und die Wärme der Sonne neigt. Es war die Jahreszeit, die häufig Not und Elend der langen Wintermonate mit sich brachte, während die Menschen eine Wiedergeburt des Jahres erwarteten.

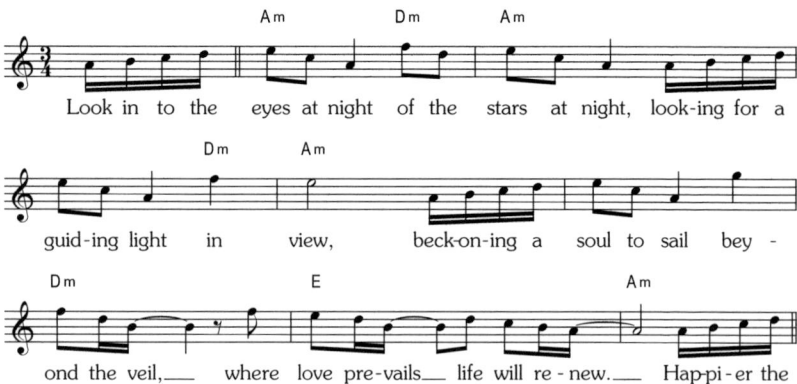

Look in to the eyes at night of the stars at night, look-ing for a
guid-ing light in view, beck-on-ing a soul to sail bey-
ond the veil,___ where love pre-vails___ life will re - new.___ Hap-pi - er the

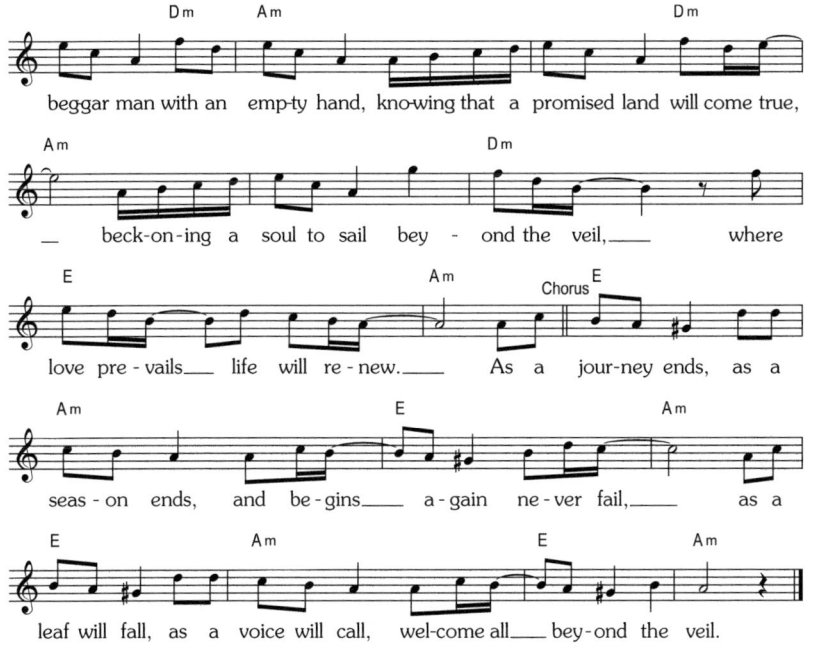

beggar man with an emp-ty hand, kno-wing that a promised land will come true,

_ beck-on-ing a soul to sail bey - ond the veil,___ where

love pre - vails___ life will re - new.___ As a jour-ney ends, as a

seas - on ends, and be - gins___ a-gain ne - ver fail,___ as a

leaf will fall, as a voice will call, wel-come all___ bey-ond the veil.

Look into the eyes at night of the stars at night,
Looking for a guiding light in view,
Beckoning a soul to sail beyond the veil,
Where love prevails life will renew.

Happier the beggar-man with an empty hand,
Knowing that a promised land will come true,
Beckoning a soul to sail beyond the veil,
Where love prevails life will renew.

Chorus:
As a journey ends, as a season ends,
And begins again never fail,
As a leaf will fall,
As a voice will call,
Welcome all beyond the veil.

There will be a time I know when our sadness goes,
Evermore lost to flow in deepest seas,

Beckoning a soul to sail beyond the veil,
Where love prevails life will renew.

Would there was a path for me from bare autumn's tree,
Bright enough for all to see some way through,
Beckoning a soul to sail beyond the veil,
Where love prevails life will renew.

As a journey ends, as a season ends,
They begin again never fail,
As a leaf will fall, so a voice will call,
Welcome all beyond the veil.

Into The Twilight

Words: William Butler Yeats
Music: Jake Walton

This is an early poem by W.B. Yeats of unrequieted love. In his twenties he fell
in love with Maud Gonne, the Irish nationalist, who repeatedly refused to marry
him. She nevertheless inspired many beautiful bitter-sweet poems which were
also influenced by his idea of romantic love.

Hier handelt es sich um ein frühes Gedicht von W.B. Yeats über unerwiderte
Liebe. In den 1920ern verliebte er sich in die irische Nationalistin Maud Gonne,
die ihn aber nicht heiraten wollte. Gleichwohl inspirierte sie zahlreiche bitter-
süße Gedichte, welche von seiner Vorstellung einer romantischen Liebe ge-
prägt waren.

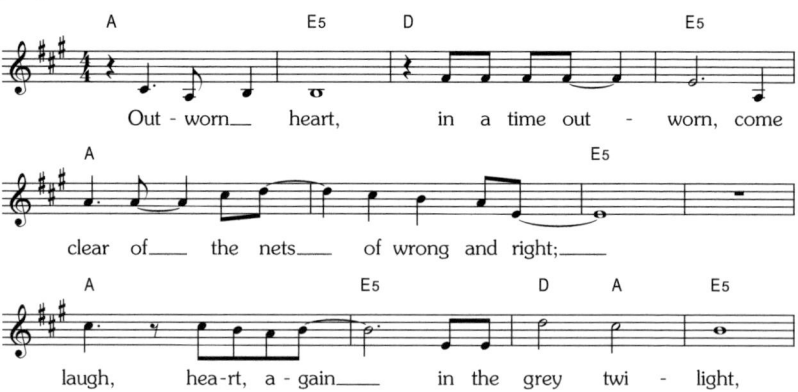

Guit. tuning: EADEAE

Out-worn heart, in a time out-worn,
Come clear of the nets of wrong and right;
Laugh, heart, again in the grey twilight,
Sigh, heart, again in the dew of the morn.

Refrain:
Your mother Eire is always young,
Dew ever shining and twilight grey;
Though hope fall from you and love decay,
Burning in fires of a slanderous tongue.

Come, heart, where hill is heaped upon hill:
For there the mystical brotherhood
Of sun and moon and hollow and wood
And river and stream work out there will.

Refrain:
And God stands winding his lonely horn,
And time and the world are ever in flight;

And love is less kind than the grey twilight,
And hope is less dear than the dew of the morn.

Out-worn heart in a time out-worn,
Come clear of the nets of wrong and right;
Laugh, heart, again in the grey twilight,
Sigh, heart, again in the dew of the morn,

Repeat:
Laugh, heart, again in the grey twilight,
Sigh, heart, again in the dew of the morn,
Sigh heart again, sigh heart again, sigh heart again,
In the dew of the morn.

The Vagabond

Words: Robert Louis Stevenson
Music: Jake Walton

Robert Louis Stevenson was born in Edinburgh, Scotland in 1850. He is probably best known for his book „Treasure Island". The Vagabond is one of his most well-known and famous poems. I have always loved the idea of a carefree, vagabond life and I did travel for a short while in a horse-drawn „Open Lot" bow wagon. These traditional wagons have no doors and are covered by a canvas sheet at the front. I remember staying on a farm where a large cat by the name of 'Big Arthur' was in charge. He and several of his friends insisted on joining me in the wagon three nights running making all attempts at sleep impossible! This was not helped by Henry the cockerel announcing the new day at 4 A.M. standing by the wagon steps, ah well, maybe the vagabond life is best left to the imagination!

Robert Louis Stevenson ist 1850 im schottischen Edinburgh geboren worden. Besonders berühmt ist er für sein Buch „Treasure Island", The Vagabond ist eines seiner bekanntesten Gedichte. Das sorgenfreie Vagabundendasein habe ich immer gemocht und eine Weile war ich selbst mit Pferd und Planwagen unterwegs. Diese traditionellen Fuhrwerke haben keine Türen und sind mit einer Baumwollplane bespannt. Ich erinnere mich, wie ich auf einer Farm rastete, auf der ein großer Kater namens Big Arthur residierte. Er und seine Kumpels bestanden darauf, mir drei Nächte lang Gesellschaft zu leisten und dabei alle Versuche vereitelten, etwas Schlaf zu finden. Daran änderte auch

74

der junge Hahn Henry nichts, wenn er um vier Uhr morgens auf dem Trittbrett den neuen Tag ankündigte. Nun gut, vielleicht sollte man das Vagabundenleben besser der Phantasie überlassen.

Guit. tuning: DADGBE

Give to me the life I love,
Let the lave go by me,
Give to me the heaven above,
And the by-way neigh me,
Bed in the bush with stars to see,
Bread I dip in the river,
That's the life for a man like me,
That's the life forever.

Let the blow fall soon or late,
Let what will be o'er me,

Give the face of earth around,
And the road before me,
Wealth I seek not hope nor love,
Nor a friend to know me,
All I seek is the heaven above,
And the road below me.

Or let autumn fall on me,
While a-field I linger,
Silencing bird on tree,
Biting blue finger,
White as meal the frosty field,
Warm the fireside haven,
Not to autumn will I yield,
Not to winter even.

Let the blow fall soon or late,
Let what will be o'er me,
Give the face of earth around,
And the road before me,
Wealth I ask not, hope nor love,
Nor a friend to know me.
All I ask's the heaven above,
And the road below me.

Give to me the life I love,
Let the lave go by me,
Give to me the heaven above,
And the by-way neigh me.

Celtic Benediction

Words: trad. / Jake Walton
Music: Jake Walton

This song is an adaptation of an old Gaelic prayer. I have heard many versions over the years where it has been used in Cornish churches. I set it to this melody and added the second verse one Christmas spent in Cornwall in the early 1980's.

Bei diesem Lied handelt es sich um die Adaption eines alten gälischen Gebets. Im Verlauf der Jahre sind mir eine ganze Reihe Versionen untergekommen, die in den Kirchen Cornwalls gesprochen werden. Eine davon habe ich in den frühen 1980er Jahren an Weihnachten vertont und durch eine zweite Strophe ergänzt.

Guit. tuning: DADGBE

Deep peace of the running wave to you,
Deep peace of the flowing air,
Deep peace of the quiet earth to you,
Deep peace of the shining star,
Deep peace of the son of peace to you,
For now and evermore.

Deep peace of the grey west wind to you,
Deep peace of the clear grey dew,
Deep peace of the soft rain to you,
Deep peace of the sky pure blue,
Deep peace of the pale white moon to you,
Peace to you.

Repeat first verse.

Emain

Words & Music: Jake Walton

This song is based on a very old story, dating back to the seventh century. In it a mysterious woman from the Otherworld appears to King Bran and his company. She brings with her a silver blossomed branch of the sacred tree from her island Emain, where there is no sickness, sorrow or death and calls them all away to her home. She is the White Goddess, which Robert Graves writes about in his book of the same name. I think that sometimes these old myths can awaken our unconscious imagination and take us on our own inner voyage.

Dieses Lied beruht auf einer sehr alten Sage aus dem siebten Jahrhundert. Darin erscheint dem König Bran und seinem Gefolge eine geheimnisvolle Frau aus der Sagenwelt. Sie führt einen mit silbernen Blüten bestandenen Ast des heimlichen Baumes ihrer Insel Emain mit sich, wo es weder Krankheit noch Sorgen oder Tod gibt, und ruft sie in ihre Welt. Es handelt sich um die weiße Göttin, über die Robert Graves in seinem gleichnamigen Buch schreibt. Ich glaube, dass diese alten Mythen aus unserem Unterbewußtsein kommen und uns auf eine eigene Reise in unser Innerstes mitnehmen können.

Pre Verse, 1st time only

Waking from my dream I saw,
Strange figure in the dawn,

With a branch of the apple bough, in her hand,
The woman sang, from the unknown land,
Silver branches hanging down,
Pure white blossom to the ground.

Chorus
Across crystal clear seas,
A land it calls to me
The unknown land.

Far away the distant shores, no sorrow knows,
Fair winds blow, healing flows,
Rain there falls in coloured showers,
It's there the birds they call the hours.

Chorus
Land of the sacred tree,
A land it calls to me
The unknown land.

And the song that the woman sang, not all could hear,
Though notes fell clear, in still air,
Yet her soft words wisdom told,
Of the far land lost so old.

Chorus
Land of the sacred tree,
Her land it calls to me
The unknown land.

With a branch of the apple bough, in her hand,
The woman sang, from the unknown land,
And with her music in the night,
Soon she faded from our sight.

Chorus
Across crystal clear seas,
Her land it calls to me
The unknown land,
The unknown land.

Lyric

Words: Mary Stewart
Music: Jake Walton

This poem comes from the collection in the book „Frost On The Window"
(Hodder and Staughton) by Mary Stewart the novelist, who is well known for
her trilogy of books on the life of Merlin the magician. Her love of natural
beauty and communion to nature is well reflected here, which inspired me to
set it to music.

Dieses Gedicht stammt aus der bei Hodder & Staughton erschienenen Antho-
logie „Frost On The Window" der Schriftstellerin Mary Stewart, die für ihre
Trilogie über das Leben des Zauberers Merlin bekannt ist. Die vorzügliche
Reflektion ihrer Liebe und Affinität zur Schönheit der Natur hat mich inspiriert, es zu vertonen.

Guit. tuning: DGDGCD

Dew shook from the wild___ rose,___ light shook from___
_ the wing, the bro-ken note___ of the wi - ld___ bird___
fell___ di - mi-nish - ing.___

Refrain
'Why do___ you___ weep?' cried___ the wi - ld___ bird,___
'to hear me sing?'___ hear the wild bi - rd sing,___
hear the wild bird sing.___

Dew Shook from the wild rose,
Light shook from the wing,
The broken note of the wild bird
Fell diminishing.

Refrain:
'Why do you weep?' cried the wild bird,
'To hear me sing?'
Hear the wild bird sing, hear the wild bird sing.

The night was pinned with white stars
Like braids of a queen's hair.
Starlight wavered and faded
Under the moon's stare.

Refrain:
'Why do you sleep?' cried the white stars,
'And the night so fair?'
And the night so fair and the night so fair.

Double Refrain:
'Why do you weep?' cried the wild bird,
'To hear me sing?'
Hear the wild bird sing.
'Why do you sleep?' cried the white stars,
'And the night so fair?'
And the night so fair and the night so fair.

Appleby Gallop

Music: Jez Lowe & Jake Walton

The Hurdy-Gurdy found me first on the Parisian folk scene during a tour with
Roger Nicholson in the 1970's. I instantly determined to try to learn to play
one and I have been trying ever since! I thought it would be interesting to
include one instrumental in this collection of songs and so have chosen this.
Jez Lowe and I included a version of it, arranged for Cittern and two Hurdy-
Gurdies (oh no!) as a bonus track on the 2001 CD re-release of „Two A
Roue". It is named after the Westmoreland town famous for it's annual horse
fair.

Die Drehleier habe ich erstmals in der Pariser Folkszene während einer Tour mit Roger Nicholson für mich entdeckt. Ich beschloss sofort, ihr Spiel zu erlernen und das tue ich immer noch. Ich denke, es wäre ganz gut, in diese Liedersammlung ein Instrumentalwerk einzufügen. Jez Lowe und ich haben eine Stück für Cittern und zwei Drehleiern (oh je) als Bonustrack für unsere 2001 wiederveröffentlichte CD „Two A Roue" aufgenommen. Es ist nach dem berühmten jährlichen Pferderennen von Westmoreland benannt.

The Spinning Of The Wheel

Words & Music: Jake Walton / Jez Lowe

When I first met Roger Nicholson at the Peelers Folk Club in north London in the early 1970's and heard him play the Appalachian Dulcimer, I was immediately captivated by its sound. It was not long after our first meeting that I started to learn the instrument. I used it to accompany the traditional song „Dance With Me" and this went on to become a staple of my repertoire in those early days. It was many years later that Jez Lowe suggested this setting where new verses acted as a counterpoint to the original, which for me has given that old favourite another lease of life. We recorded this new version, with Dulcimer and Cittern on the CD re-release of „Two A Roue" in 2001.

Als ich in den frühen 1970er Jahren Roger Nicholson im Peelers Folkclub im Norden Londons begegnete und ihn den Appalachen-Dulcimer spielen hörte, war sich sofort von dessen Klang fasziniert. Nicht lange nach unserem ersten Zusammentreffen begann ich damit, dieses Instrument zu erlernen. Ich verwendete es zur Begleitung des traditionellen Liedes „Dance With Me" und es wurde einem Angelpunkt meines damaligen Repertoires. Jez Lowe schlug viele Jahre später diese Fassung vor, in der neue Verse als Kontrapunkt zum Original fungieren, was meines Erachtens meinem alten Favoriten neues Leben einhaucht. Wir spielten diese neue Version im Jahre 2001 für die Wiederveröffentlichung unseres Albums „Two A Roue" ein.

Melody:
Oh dance with me my charming one,
With your golden, golden slippers on,
Will you dance with me my charming one,
With your golden, golden slippers on?

Melody:
I'll buy you silken hose to wear,
I'll buy ribbons all for your hair,
The sun and moon for you I'll steal,
If you dance with me my Mary Neil.

Counterpart:
A lilting rhyme is not a promise,
A lilting tune is not a stone written pledge,
A merry dance is not a token,
A silken heart spun in fine golden thread.

Melody:
I'll buy for you a gown of green,
The purest thread you've ever seen,
You'll be fairer than a queen,
If you'll dance with me my Mary Neil.

Counterpart:
Better promises have been broken,
Better pledges lost in a moment of time,
Better words have faded forgotten,
But never a heart more shattered then scattered like mine.

Melody:
Grab your hands and make our reel,
All together now hear them sing,
We're going to dance the Sligo reel,
And I'd love to dance with Mary Neil.

Counterpart:
Did your kiss not seal such a promise,
Did your voice not sing loudest of love all along,
Did your eyes not shine bright in the morning,
Did your heart not beat loud at the lilt of the song.

Silver Muse

Words: trad. / Jake Walton
Music: Jake Walton

An old Celtic blessing to the new moon of the season inspired this song. The lunar Celtic goddess Arianrhod was known as the „Lady of the Silver Wheel". It was she who held the threads of life and the quest for her castle was a quest for immortality. This quest has also been associated with other Celtic voyages to the Otherworld, such as the story of Emain.

Inspiriert ist dieses Lied von einer alten keltischen Segnung des Neumonds. Die keltische Mondgöttin Ananrhod war als „Lady of the Silver Wheel" geläufig. Sie hielt die Lebensfäden in der Hand und die Suche nach ihrem Schloß war so etwas wie das Streben nach Unsterblichkeit. Wie in der Geschichte von Emain wurde diese Suche auch mit Reisen ins Jenseits der Kelten assoziiert.

Intro / Link: G / D7

Thou fair moon of the season, thou great lamp of grace.

Refrain:
May your light be fair to me,
May your light be clear to me,
May your course be true.

Thou fair moon of the season, thou great lamp of grace.

Verse:
If good to me is your begining, as your wheel turns to the sky,
Better by seven be your ending, as you hold the threads of life.

Refrain:
May your light be fair to me,
May your light be clear to me,
May your course be true.

Chorus:
Silver moon, slender moon,
Silver muse of the night.

Thou fair moon of the season, thou great lamp of grace.

Verse:
I lift my eye to you each evening, Queen of starry dark skies,
I raise my hand to you in greeting, as you steer the silvery tide.

Refrain:
May your light be fair to me,
May your light be clear to me,
May your course be true.

Chorus:
Silver moon, slender moon,
Silver muse of the night,
Silver muse of the night.

By The Margin Of The Great Deep

Words: George Russell
Music: Jake Walton

George Russell (1867 – 1935) was a poet, author and mystical friend of
W.B.Yeats. His first book of verse was called „Homeward – Songs by the Way"
and this poem for me contains a certain longing of the spirit for homecoming.
It is a type of homesickness, but different to that sometimes expressed in the
poetry of Walter de la Mare for instance, which is often a longing for things
past. The poem certainly evokes a great sense of peace. I tried to reflect this in
the melody, which was also inspired by the evening skies of Cornwall.

George Russell (1867 – 1935) war ein Poet, Schriftsteller und erklärter An-
hänger von W.B. Yeats. Sein erster Gedichtband trug den Titel „Homeward -

Songs by the Way". Dieses Gedicht daraus verkörpert für mich die Sehnsucht nach der Rückkehr in die Heimat. Es ist eine Form von Heimweh, aber anders, als sie beispielsweise in der Poesie von Walter de la Mare zum Ausdruck kommt, die häufig eine Sehnsucht nach der Vergangenheit ausdrückt. Das Gedicht strahlt ein Gefühl von Frieden aus, das ich mit meiner Melodie unterstreichen wollte, die von der Abendstimmung in Cornwall inspiriert worden ist.

Guit. tuning: EADEAE Capo 2nd Fret; Play ( ) Chords

being as o' - er___ fills the heart with awe,

grow - ing one_____ with its si - lent stream.

When the breath of twilight blows to flame the misty skies,
All its vaporous sapphire, violet glow and silver gleam,
With their magic flood me through the gateway of the eyes,
I am one with the twilight's dream.

When the trees skies and fields are one in dusky mood,
Every heart of man is rapt within the mother's breast,
Full of peace and sleep and dreams in the vasty quietude,
I am one with their hearts at rest.

Chorus:
Aye and deep and deep and deeper let me drink and draw,
From the olden fountain more than light or peace or dream,
Such primeval being as o'erfills the heart with awe,
Growing one with its silent stream.

From our immemorial joys of hearth and home and love,
Strayed away along the margin of the unknown tide,
All its reach of soundless calm can thrill me far above,
Word or touch from the lips beside.

(Chorus)

Aye and deep and deep and deeper let me drink and draw,
Growing one with its silent stream,
I am one with the twilight's dream,
Growing one with its silent stream.

The Plain Of Silver

Words: Jake Walton
Music: Eric Liorzou

In Celtic legend The Plain of Silver was the land of enchantment and inspiration, which was entered at twilight, when tales and stories were told as darkness fell. One of the aims of those old songs and poems was to bring peace and healing to the soul, with this song I tried to follow in that tradition.

In keltischen Legenden war The Plain of Silver das Land des Zaubers und der Inspiration, welches sich in der Dämmerung offenbarte, wenn bei Einbruch der Dunkelheit Märchen und Sagen erzählt wurden. Ein Zweck solcher alten Lieder und Gedichte war die Beförderung von Frieden und Seelenheil. An diese Überlieferung wollte ich mit meinem Lied anknüpfen.

A wind is on the moor - land, moon-light's on the sea,—

tra - vell-er's in the fire - light, by sha-dow of the tree.

Far from the tro-bles of the world and far from the ways of men,

tra-vell-er lights his fi - re in the dark-ness of the glen,

search for the plain of sil - ver and rest for the wea - ry soul,

search for the plain of sil-ver.

A wind is on the moorland,
Moonlight's on the sea,
Traveller's in the firelight,
By shadow of the tree.

Chorus:
Far from the troubles of the world,
And far from the ways of men,
Traveller lights his fire,
In the darkness of the glen,
Search for the plain of silver,
And rest for the weary soul,
Search for the plain of silver.

When the hare's to the moon at twilight,
He'll watch for the way alone,
Traveller's in the starlight,
Close by standing stone.

(Chorus)

The eagle sails the hillside,
Salmon swims in the burn,
The stag he rests in the half-light,
From these the heart will learn.

(Chorus)

Traveller stands in silence,
Close to the earth and tree,
Part of the wind and star-shine,
Traveller's alone and free.

(Chorus)

Peat Fire

Words: J. Kett
Music: Jake Walton

Often friends give me poems, suggesting that I try and set them to music. I am not always successful in my efforts but if the poem resonates in some way with me I usually get some ideas for a melody. In this case the words reminded me of Scotland in the autumn which is always a beautiful time of the year.

Häufig bekomme ich von Feunden Gedichte mit der Empfehlung, diese zu vertonen. Nicht immer wird etwas draus, aber wenn ein Gedicht auf meinen Nerv trifft, kommen mir doch ein paar Ideen für eine Melodie in den Sinn. In diesem Fall erinnerte mich der Text an den schottischen Herbst, der eine wunderschöne Jahreszeit ist.

Intro: D add9

We gazed at the glow talked of fa-mil-iar things as to-ge-ther we sat, by the fi-re of peat with the col-lie, her head on paws a-sleep at our feet the night our thoughts to-ok wing. the night our tho-ughts took wing, the night our thoughts to-ok wing.

We gazed at the glow, talked of familiar things,
As together we sat, by the fire of peat,
With the collie, her head on paws asleep at our feet,
The night our thoughts took wing.

Outside the heather and cotton grass covered the hill,
Far to the north, a mirror of sea for miles,
As the evening was bringing its peace to the lovely isle,
But the air was chill.

For the year had turned, welcome was the heat,
Life's fast pace eased, time for a while stood still,
And long we'll remember that night, the heather, the hill
And the warm glow of the peat.

Repeat:
And long we'll remember that night, the heather, the hill
And the warm glow of the peat.

Refrain:
The night our thoughts took wing,
The night our thoughts took wing.

Tom O'Bedlam's Dream

Words: trad.
Music: Jake Walton

This is a truly heartfelt poem about the matters that are the source of poetry. Bedlam was originally the name of a hospital for the insane and Tom O'Bedlam became the traditional name for a fool or „Village idiot". Robert Graves, in his book „The White Goddess", considers the poem to have been inspired by the muse and that love of the Goddess or muse makes the poet mad causing his „death", which in turn enables him to regain his wits and become wise. Tom's habit is to watch the night sky. The birds of the night are his body and emotions. He knows more than the sun (Apollo) because he knows of the dark. He sees the planets Venus (the Queen of Love) and Mars (the Warrior). He encounters a Knight (the night?) with his horse (Pegasus) and spear (Sagittarius) and comes face to face with life and death, light and darkness. This to him now is no problem, he is indifferent to either and a free spirit.

Hier handelt es sich um ein wahrlich tiefsinniges Gedicht über den Quell aller Poesie. Bedlam war eigentlich der Name einer Irrenanstalt und Tom O'Bedlam war traditionell die Bezeichnung für Verrückte oder Dorfdeppen. Robert Graves Buch „The White Goddes" beschreibt das Gedicht als von der Muse inspiriert, die den Poeten in den Wahnsinn treibt und ihm mit dem damit verbundenen Todeserlebnis eine Erneuerung seines Verstandes und Weisheit verschafft. Tom pflegt den nächtlichen Sternenhimmel zu betrachten. Wobei die Vögel der Nacht seinen Leib und seine Gefühle verkörpern. Er kennt mehr als die Sonne (Apollo), weil er um das Dunkel weiß. Er erblickt die Planeten Venus (die Liebesgöttin) und Mars (den Kriegsgott). Er begegnet einem Ritter mit Pferd (Sternbild Pegasus) und Speer (Sternbild Schütze) und sieht sich Leben und Tod, Licht und Finsternis ausgesetzt. Über den Dingen stehend und als Freigeist spielt das für ihn nun keine Rolle mehr.

Guit. tuning: DADGAD

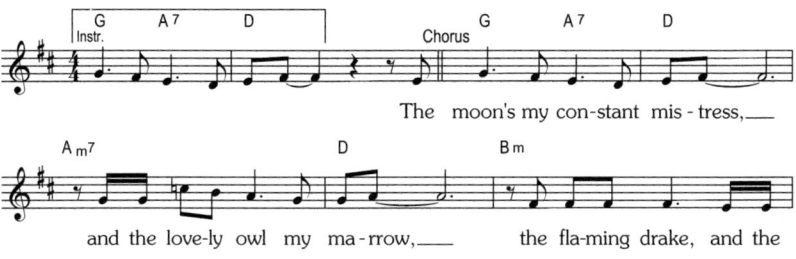

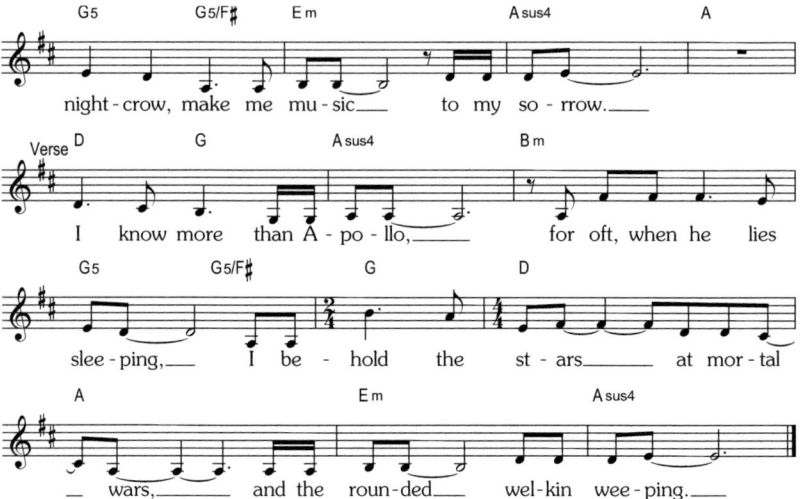

night - crow, make me mu - sic___ to my so - rrow.___

I know more than A - po - llo,___ for oft, when he lies

slee - ping,___ I be - hold the st - ars___ at mor - tal

___ wars,___ and the roun-ded___ wel-kin wee - ping.___

Chorus:
The moon's my constant mistress,
And the lovely owl my marrow,
The flaming drake,
And the night-crow, make
Me music to my sorrow.

Verse:
I know more than Apollo,
For oft, when he lies sleeping,
I behold the stars
At mortal wars,
And the rounded welkin weeping.

Verse:
The moon embraces her shepherd,
And the Queen of Love her warrior;
While the first does horn
The stars of the morn,
And the next the heavenly farrier.

Chorus:
The moon's my constant mistress,
And the lovely owl my marrow,

100

The flaming drake,
And the night-crow, make
Me music to my sorrow.

Verse:
With a heart of furious fancies,
Whereof I am commander:
With a burning spear,
And a horse of air,
To the wilderness I wander.

Verse:
With a Knight of ghosts and shadows,
I summoned am to Tourney,
Ten leagues beyond The wild world's end;
Methinks it is no journey.

Chorus

Repeat:
The flaming drake,
And the night-crow, make
Me music to my sorrow,
For the moon's my constant mistress.

White Wave Sea

Words: trad. / Jake Walton
Music: Jake Walton

This song was based on a fragment of an early Irish poem. It sums up for me the Celtic monk's affinity to nature and the interrelatedness of all life, which we would now call ecology.

Grundlage dieses Liedes ist ein altes irisches Gedicht. Für mich fasst es die Affinität der keltischen Mönche zur Natur und der Wechselwirkung alles Lebens zusammen. Heute würden wir das als Ökologie bezeichnen.

To the ma-ker___ of all things,___ Lord wor-ship we,

hea-ven white with an - gels' wings, earth and white wave sea.

Earth and wh-ite___ wave___ sea.

Hea-ven white with an - gels' wings ov - er,___ white wave___ sea,___ hea-ven white with an - gels' wings ov - er,___ white wave___ sea.

To the maker of all things,
Lord worship we,
Heaven white with angels' wings,
Earth and white wave sea.
Earth and white wave sea.

To the north the star of hope,
To the east the spring,
From the south the summer comes,
West the autumn brings,
Bright autumn brings.

Interlude:
To the maker of all things,
Lord worship we,
Heaven white with angels' wings,
Earth and white wave sea,
Earth and white wave sea.

Coda:
Heaven white with angels' wings over,
White wave sea,
Heaven white with angels' wings over,
White wave sea.

Outro

by Jake Walton

I've always loved songs and singing. For most of us growing up in England in the 1950s the radio was the main source of music. I remember the weekday BBC programme "Housewives' Choice" where Bing Crosby, Doris Day, and many others could be heard. I had a little red plastic guitar when I was 4 years old; but it was only a toy and it wasn't until many years later that I'd become the proud owner of a cherry red Gibson J-45. By the late 1950s Radio Luxembourg was the station to listen to and rock & roll was inspiring many young bands all over the country. I took up the drums and began playing in several groups. In one band the singer used to perform great Elvis impersonations. He was also writing a musical at the time. I recall, while chatting to him one night, I said I thought that he should concentrate on a singing career rather than musicals. The following year Jesus Christ Superstar opened in London and I realised that the singer I'd been speaking to the year before had been none other than Tim Rice. Well I got that wrong!

It was the early albums of Bert Jansch and Donovan however, that had opened up the world of the acoustic guitar for many of my generation, including myself. I concentrated on learning to play "fingerstyle" guitar and by the late 1960s had started playing in Cornish folk clubs, but was still drumming with a heavy blues band, "Graphite" back in Reading where I was at university. On one memorable occasion we supported Hawkwind but by the early 1970s (whilst teaching guitar in London) a chance meeting at the "Peeler's" folk club with dulcimer player Roger Nicholson, was to take me in a very different direction. Roger was looking for someone to accompany him, so after a few rehearsals together I found myself touring clubs in the UK and on the continent. I was also learning to play the dulcimer and a partnership was to develop that lasted several years. On one tour in America, I was fortunate enough to meet Jean Ritchie the renowned singer and dulcimer player from Kentucky. Her family's collection of old ballads although often tinged with a melancholy, had great strength, beauty and purity. The dulcimer with its medieval looks and modal sound had caught my imagination. I found it worked well on ballads such as Lamachree and Megrum. I also used it almost exclusively on the Lazy Farmer LP when in the band with Wizz Jones in the mid-1970s.

I have many fond memories of those times living in London. I was sharing a flat with John Bidwell (ex C.O.B.) who was also a member of Lazy Farmer; and much socialising was done at the Half Moon pub in Putney. I remember one day spent in the company of Bert Jansch and some friends. On leaving the pub late that evening I managed to walk straight into a brick wall. John Bidwell picked me up off the pavement and on reaching the Indian restaurant just down the road, the first thing Bert did was to pour me a large glass of wine as blood dripped from a gash in my forehead. That day he inadvertently warned me of falling prey to some of the prevalent excesses of the time! "Never again" I thought; but I will never forget his friendship, kindness and encouragement. He had just released his "Moonshine" album at the time and the title track still remains one of my all-time favourite songs. He's left us with a wonderful legacy of music.

When visiting a club in Paris on another tour with Roger Nicholson I first heard the hurdy gurdy. The French call it a "vielle à roue" or "fiddle with a wheel". I was captivated. Having long been interested in the music of the troubadours and minstrels of 13 th century France the sound of the hurdy gurdy was like a homecoming. The instrument had died out in the UK.. I wonder why ?! Nevertheless I soon managed to get the name of a French maker, Christian Laborie, who lived in the foothills of the Alps. One January morning in 1975 after finishing a tour of Brittany, I set off to find him in my Citroen 2CV. Three days later I arrived. Christian, apart from making hurdy gurdies, was also building his house at the time. I spent that night on a concrete floor next to a large hole in the wall and nearly froze. Undaunted; the next day I ordered a guitar shaped hurdy gurdy based on a classical Saunier model. The following year I collected my finished gurdy and started to learn to play it. The instrument with its thousand year history covering both middle and Eastern Europe provided inspiration for many songs some of which I've included in this collection. I used it a great deal when touring both with Jez Lowe and Eric Liorzou in the 1980s.

Another source of material for me has been the mystic poets like W.B Yeats and George Russell (A.E) as well as others long forgotten who have passed on Celtic myth and legend. Take for instance the story of Tom O' Bedlam, who was driven insane by his love for the muse; yet she destroys only to quicken and having confronted the dark side of his psyche he becomes wise. He is an archetype of the wounded healer. In the song Plain of Silver I used the myth of the hare as a messenger, bringing back the meditative stillness and intuition of the moon's reflected light. Another example is the beautiful old legend of Emain which echoes the Celtic people's deep desire to penetrate the otherworld. These stories help me to reconnect and remember the time before we lost touch with the „unseen".

In any event, I hope that some of these songs (which cover a cross section of my repertoire spanning four decades) may act as a catalyst or inspiration for the reader on their own musical journeys; and if nothing else may offer the chance to dream ...

A wind is on the moorland,
Moonlight's on the sea,
Traveller's in the firelight,
By shadow of the tree.

Outro

von Jake Walton

Lieder und Gesang habe ich schon immer geliebt. Für die meisten von uns, die in den 1950er Jahren aufgewachsen sind, war das Radio die vornehmlichste Quelle für Musik. Ich erinnere mich an das wöchentliche BBC Programm „Housewives' Choice", wo man Bing Crosby, Doris Day und viele andere hören konnte. Als ich vier Jahre alt war, besaß ich eine kleine rote Plastikgitarre; es war nur ein Spielzeug und erst viele Jahre später wurde ich stolzer Besitzer einer kirschroten Gibson J 45. In den späten 1950er Jahren galt Radio Luxemburg als der angesagteste Sender und Rock ‚n' Roll war für viele junge Bands im ganzen Land eine Inspiration. Ich entschied mich fürs Schlagzeug und begann in diversen Gruppen zu spielen. In einer der Bands hatte der Sänger tolle Elvis-Imitationen drauf. Damals arbeitete er auch an einem Musical. Ich erinnere mich, dass ich ihm eines Nachts bei einem Schwatz riet, sich mehr auf seine Sänger-Karriere zu konzentrieren. Im folgenden Jahr kam in London „Jesus Christ Superstar" heraus und ich begriff, dass der Sänger, mit dem ich ein Jahr zuvor geredet hatte, kein geringerer als Tim Rice war. Ich lag mit meinen Ratschlägen also ziemlich daneben.

Für mich und viele andere meiner Generation eröffneten die frühen Alben von Bert Jansch die Welt der akustischen Gitarre. Ich konzentrierte mich darauf, das Fingerpicking-Spiel zu erlernen und begann in den späten 1960er Jahren damit in Folkclubs in Cornwall aufzutreten, spielte aber auch noch Schlagzeug in der Blues-Band Graphite in Reading, wo ich an der Uni studierte. Bei einer denkwürdigen Gelegenheit begleiteten wir sogar die Gruppe Hawkwind. Doch in den frühen 1970er Jahren, als ich in London als Gitarrenlehrer lebte, lenkte mich ein zufälliges Zusammentreffen mit dem Dulcimer-Spieler Roger Nicholson im Peeler's Folkclub in eine ganz andere Richtung. Roger war gerade auf der Suche nach einer Begleitung. Und nach ein paar gemeinsamen Proben befand ich mich schon auf Tournee durch die Clubs des Vereinigten Königreichs und des Kontinents. Ich erlernte den Dulcimer zu spielen und es entwickelte sich eine langjährige Partnerschaft. Anlässlich einer Amerika-Tour hatte ich das Glück, die berühmte Sängerin und Dulcimer Spielerin Jean Ritchie aus Kentucky kennenzulernen. Wenn auch häufig von einer melancholischen Färbung, besitzt ihr Fundus aus alten Balladen eine enorme Kraft, Schönheit und Reinheit. Mit seiner mittelalterlichen Anmutung und seinem typischen Klang hat mich der Dulcimer in seinen Bann gezogen. Er passt meines Erachtens bestens zu Balladen wie „Lamarchree And Megrum". Mitte der 1970er Jahre verwendete ich ihn auch für die LP von Wizz Jones Band Lazy Farmer.

An meine Londoner Zeiten denke ich sehr gern zurück. Damals teilte ich mir eine Wohnung mit John Bidwell, der ebenfalls Mitglied von Lazy Farmer war. (Bekannt geworden durch die Mitwirkung in Clive's Original Band / C.O.B.

des Incredible String Band Musikers Clive Palmer. Anm. des Übersetzers). Mit Freunden haben wir uns seinerzeit häufig im Half Mood Pub in Putney getroffen. Ich erinnere mich, wie wir dort einen Tag mit Bert Jansch verbrachten. Als ich am Abend den Pub verließ, knallte ich schnurstracks gegen eine Mauer. John Bidwell half mir auf und nachdem wir ein indisches Restaurant weiter runter in der Straße erreicht hatten, spendierte Bert mir ein großes Glas Wein, während das Blut über meine Stirn rann. Damals hat er mich eindringlich gewarnt, künftig Exzesse dieser Art zu meiden. „Das war das letzte Mal" dachte ich bei mir. Seine Freundlichkeit und Ermutigung sind mir unvergesslich geblieben. Er hatte gerade sein Moonshine Album vollendet, dessen Titelsong zu meinen ewigen Favoriten gehört. Im verdanken wir ein großartiges musikalisches Erbe.

Bei einem Besuch eines Clubs in Paris während einer weiteren Tournee mit Roger Nicholson kam mir erstmals eine Drehleier zu Gehör. Die Franzosen nennen sie „Vielle à roue" oder Geige mit Rad. Ich war sofort verzaubert. Schon lange an der Musik und den Gesängen französischer Troubadoure interessiert, erschien mir die Drehleier wie eine Offenbarung. In Groß Britannien ist dieses Instrument zu gut wie ausgestorben. Keine Ahnung warum. Aber wie dem auch sei, ich stieß bald auf den Namen des französischen Instrumentebauers Christian Labonie, welcher in den Ausläufern der Alpen lebte. Eines Morgens im Januar 1975 nach einer Tournee durch die Bretagne brach ich mit meinen Citroen 2 CV auf und drei Tage später erreichte ich mein Ziel. Seinerzeit war Christian neben der Fertigung von Drehleiern auch mit dem Bau seines Hauses beschäftigt. Ich verbrachte die Nacht in dessen Rohbau vor einer großen Maueröffnung und frohr gewaltig. Beherzt gab ich am nächsten Tag eine Drehleier in Auftrag, die auf dem klassischen Saunier Modell basierte. Ein Jahr später holte ich dann meine fertige Drehleier ab und begann sofort, ihre Handhabung zu erlernen. Dieses Instrument mit seiner gut tausend jährigen mittel- und osteuropäischen Geschichte hat viele der Lieder beeinflusst, die ich in meine Sammlung aufgenommen habe. Auf meinen Tourneen mit Jez Lowe kam sie immer wieder zum Einsatz.

Eine weitere Quelle waren für mich mystische Gedichte von Poeten wie W.B.Yeats, George Russell oder anderen langst vergessenen Autoren, die auf den Pfaden der keltischen Mythen und Legenden gewandelt sind. Man nehme zum Beispiel die Geschichte von Tom O'Bedlam, der von seiner Liebe zur Muse in den Wahnsinn getrieben wurde. Aber sie zerstörte nur, um etwas Neues zu erschaffen, und ihn in einen weisen Mann verwandelte, nachdem sie ihn mit den dunklen Seiten seiner Seele konfrontiert hatte. Er ist ein Urbild des verwundeten Heilers. Im Lied „Plain Of Silver" benutze ich die Legende vom Hasen als Botschafter, der die meditative Ruhe und Einfühlungsgabe in Erinnerung ruft, die im Mondlicht schimmert. Ein anderes Beispiel ist die wunderschöne alte Sage von Emain, welche die tiefe Sehnsucht des keltischen Volkes nach dem Verständnis der jenseitigen Welt zum Ausdruck bringt. Solche Geschichten helfen mir ein Gespür für jene Zeiten zu entwickeln, als wir unseren Bezug zur unsichtbaren Wirklichkeit des Jenseits noch nicht verloren hatten. Wie dem auch sei, ich hoffe dass diese Lieder aus einer über vier Jahrzehnte reichenden Schaffensperiode dazu inspirieren eigene musikalische Reisen zu unternehmen. Und wenn sich keine andere Gelegenheit zum Träumen ergeben sollte, dann ...

A wind is on the moorland,
Moonlight's on the sea,
Traveller's in the firelight,
By shadow of the tree.

Sincere thanks to all the musicians and singers known and unknown for the inspiration, they have given. Thanks to John Davison for all his work on the Transcriptions, Vivien Nicholson for the beautiful artwork and Jez Lowe for his kind words. Many thanks also to Erin and Bryony Holden for their encouragement, help and support.

Jake Walton

The Works / Die Werke

The Music Makers. Copyright © Jake Walton & Bucks Music Ltd. For Germany, Austria & Switzerland: Heupferd Musik Verlag GmbH GmbH. Rel.: „Jake Walton – Sunlight And Shade" (Folkfreak LP FF 4012). Rec. 1982, rel. 1983. „Jake Walton – Songs From The Gurdy Man" (Wundertüte / Klangwelten CD TÜT JW 72.1990). Rel. 1990. Jake Walton (Vocals, Guitar), Eric Liorzou (Guitar), Stephen Cooney (Lead Guitar, Bass Guitar).

The Gloaming Grey. Copyright © Jake Walton & Bucks Music Ltd. For Germany, Austria & Switzerland: Heupferd Musik Verlag GmbH. Rel.: „Jake Walton – The Gloaming Grey" (Folkfreak LP FF 4001). Rec. & rel. 1979. Jake Walton (Hurdy Gurdy, Guitar, Vocals), Emanuel Pariselle (Whistle).

After The Plough. Copyright © Jake Walton & Bucks Music Ltd. For Germany, Austria & Switzerland: Heupferd Musik Verlag GmbH. Copyright Words © Elisabeth J. Coatsworth. Rel.: „Roger Nicholson / Jake Walton / Andrew Cronshaw – Times & Traditions For The Dulcimer" (Trailer LP LER 2094). Rec. & Rel. 1976. Jake Walton (Vocals, Dulcimer).

The Bonny Labouring Boy. Copyright © Jake Walton & Bucks Music Ltd. For Germany, Austria & Switzerland: Heupferd Musik Verlag GmbH. Rel.: „Jake Walton – The Gloaming Grey" (Folkfreak LP 4001). Rec. & rel. 1979. Jake Walton (Guitar, Vocals).

Lamachree And Megrum. Copyright © Jake Walton & Bucks Music Ltd. For Germany, Austria & Switzerland: Heupferd Musik Verlag GmbH. Rel.: „Jake Walton – The Gloaming Grey" (Folkfreak LP FF 4001). Rec. & rel. 1979. Jake Walton (Dulcimer, Vocals), Emanuel Pariselle (Concertina, Whistle).

Bogie's Bonny Belle. Copyright © Jake Walton & Bucks Music Ltd. For Germany, Austria & Switzerland: Heupferd Musik Verlag GmbH. Rel.: „Roger Nicholson / Jake Walton / Andrew Cronshaw – Times & Traditions For The Dulcimer" (Trailer LP LER 2094). Rec. & Rel. 1976. Jake Walton (Vocals, Guitar), Roger Nicholson (Dulcimer).

The Gypsy's Wedding Day. Copyright © Jake Walton & Bucks Music Ltd. For Germany, Austria & Switzerland: Heupferd Musik Verlag GmbH. Rel.: „Roger Nicholson / Jake Walton / Andrew Cronshaw – Times & Traditions For The Dulcimer" (Trailer LP LER 2094). Rec. & Rel. 1976. Jake Walton (Vocals, Guitar).

The Beggarman. Copyright © Jake Walton & Bucks Music Ltd. For Germany, Austria & Switzerland: Heupferd Musik Verlag GmbH. Rel. „Jake Walton – The Gloaming Grey" (Folkfreak LP FF 4001). Rec. & rel. 1979. Jake Walton (Guitar, Hurdy Gurdy, Vocals), Emanuel Pariselle (Bodhran).

Sunlight And Shade. Copyright © Jake Walton & Bucks Music Ltd. For Germany, Austria & Switzerland: Heupferd Musik Verlag GmbH. Rel.: „Jake Walton – Sunlight And Shade" (Folkfreak LP FF 4012). Rec. 1982, rel. 1983. „Jake Walton – Songs

From The Gurdy Man" (Wundertüte / Klangwelten CD TÜT JW 72.1990). Rel. 1990. Jake Walton (Vocals, Guitar), Eric Liorzou (Mandola, Guitar), Stephen Cooney (Bass, Mandolin), Joe McKenna (Pipes). **The Trees They Grow High**. Copyright © Jake Walton & Bucks Music Ltd. For Germany, Austria & Switzerland: Heupferd Musik Verlag GmbH. **Tristan's Song**. Copyright © Jake Walton & Bucks Music Ltd. For Germany, Austria & Switzerland: Heupferd Musik Verlag GmbH. Rel.: „Jake Walton – The Gloaming Grey" (Folkfreak LP FF 4001). Rec. & rel. 1979. Jake Walton (Guitar, Vocals). „Jake Walton – Songs From The Gurdy Man" (Wundertüte / Klangwelten CD TÜT JW 72.1990). Rec. & rel. 1990. Jake Walton (Vocals, Guitar), Eric Liorzou (Guitar), Stephen Cooney (Fretless Bass), Jo Partridge (Keyboards). **Standing Stones**. Copyright © Jake Walton & Bucks Music Ltd. For Germany, Austria & Switzerland: Heupferd Musik Verlag GmbH. Rel.: „Jake Walton – Sunlight And Shade" (Folkfreak LP FF 4012). Rec. 1982, rel. 1983. „Jake Walton – Songs From The Gurdy Man" (Wundertüte / Klangwelten CD TÜT JW 72.1990). Rel. 1990. Jake Walton (Guitar, Vocals), Eric Liorzou (Guitar), Joe McKenna (Pipes), Stephen Cooney (Bass, Didgeridoo). **Echoes**. Copyright Music © Jake Walton & Bucks Music Ltd. For Germany, Austria & Switzerland: Heupferd Musik Verlag GmbH. Copyright Words © Walter de la Mare & Society of Authors. Rel.: „Jake Walton – The Gloaming Grey" (Folkfreak LP FF 4001). Rec. & rel. 1979. Jake Walton (Dulcimer, Vocals). **The Wheel Of Fortune**. Copyright © Jez Lowe & Lowe Life Music. Rel.: „Jez Lowe – Jez Lowe" (Fellside LP FE 023). Rec. & rel. 1980. Jez Lowe (Vocals, Guitar), Sylvia Barnes (Vocals). **The Curragh Of Kildare**. Copyright © Jake Walton & Bucks Music Ltd. For Germany, Austria & Switzerland: Heupferd Musik Verlag GmbH. **The West Wind**. Copyright Music © Jake Walton & Bucks Music Ltd. Copyright Words © John Masefield & Society of Authors. Rel. „Jake Walton – Emain" (Wundertüte CD TÜT 72.180). Rec. 1999, rel. 2000. Jake Walton (Guitar, Vocals), Eric Liorzou (Mandola), Jez Lowe (Harmony Vocals), Mike O'Connor (Fiddle). **Song Of Parting**. Copyright © Jake Walton & Bucks Music Ltd. For Germany, Austria & Switzerland: Heupferd Musik Verlag GmbH. Rel. „Jake Walton – Sunlight And Shade" (Folfreak LP FF 4012). Rec. 1982, rel. 1983. „Jake Walton – Songs From The Gurdy Man" (Wundertüte / Klangwelten CD TÜT JW 72.1990). Rel. 1990. Jake Walton (Vocals, Hury Gurdy), Eric Liorzou (Guitar), Stephen Cooney (Bass). **The Quiet Lands Of Erin**. Copyright © Jake Walton & Bucks Music Ltd. For Germany, Austria & Switzerland: Heupferd Musik Verlag GmbH. Rel. „Roger Nicholson and Jake Walton – Bygone Days / Music For Dulcimer And Hurdy Gurdy" (Front Hall Records LP FHR 015). Rec. & rel. 1980. Jake Walton (Vocals, Guitar). **The Valley Lay Smiling**. Copyright © Jake Walton & Bucks Music Ltd. For Germany, Austria & Switzerland: Heupferd Musik Verlag GmbH. Rel. „Jake Walton – Sunlight And Shade" (Folfreak LP FF 4012). Rec. 1982, rel. 1983. „The Free Spirit – Music For Dulcimer" (Folkfreak LP FF 4008). Rel. 1982. „Jake Walton – Songs From The Gurdy

Man" (Wundertüte / Klangwelten CD TÜT JW 72.1990). Rel. 1990. Jake Walton (Vocals, Guitar), Eric Liorzou (Guitar).
All That's Past. Copyright Music © Jake Walton & Bucks Music Ltd. Copyright Words © Walter de La Mare & Society of Authors. Rel. „Jake Walton – Emain" (Wundertüte CD TÜT 72.180). Rec. 1999, rel. 2000. Jake Walton (Vocals, Guitar), Eric Liorzou (Guitars), Mike O'Connor (Fiddle).
Patrick's Song. Copyright © Patrick Ewen & Jake Walton. Rec. & Rel. 1986. Jez Lowe & Jake Walton – Two A Roue (Fellside LP FE 4012. Jake Walton (Vocals, Hurdy Gurdy), Jez Lowe (Cittern, Harmonica).
Black Sarah. Copyright © Lorraine A. Lee-Hammond & Snowy Egret Music. Rel. „Jake Walton – Sunlight And Shade" (Folfreak LP FF 4012). Rec. 1982, rel. 1983. Jake Walton (Hurdy Gurdy, Vocals). „Jake Walton – Songs From The Gurdy Man" (Wundertüte / Klangwelten CD TÜT JW 72.1990). Rec. 1990, rel. 1990. Jake Walton (Vocals, Hurdy Gurdy), Stephen Cooney (Didgeridoo), Eric Liorzou (Guitar, Mandola).
September Morning. Copyright © Jake Walton & Bucks Music Ltd. For Germany, Austria & Switzerland: Heupferd Musik Verlag GmbH. Rel. „Jake Walton – Sunlight And Shade" (Folfreak LP FF 4012). Rec. 1982, rel. 1983. „The Free Spirit – Music For Dulcimer" (Folkfreak LP FF 4008). Rel. 1982. Jake Walton (Guitar, Vocals), Stephen Coooney (Bass), Eric Liorzou (Bass).
Reign Of The Fair Maid. Copyright © Jake Walton & Bucks Music Ltd. For Germany, Austria & Switzerland: Heupferd Musik Verlag GmbH. „Jez Lowe & Jake Walton – Two A Roue" (Fellside Records LP FE 055). Rec. & rel. 1986. „Jake Walton – Songs From The Gurdy Man" (Wundertüte / Klangwelten CD TÜT JW 72.1990). rel. 1990. Jake Walton (Vocals, Guitar), Jez Lowe (Vocals, Cittern), Jo Partridge (Electric Guitar, Percussion).
Trees. Copyright © Jake Walton & Bucks Music Ltd. For Germany, Austria & Switzerland: Heupferd Musik Verlag GmbH. Rec. 1986. „Jez Lowe & Jake Walton – Two A Roue" (Fellside Records LP FE 055). Rel. 1986. Jake Walton – Songs From The Gurdy Man (Wundertüte / Klangwelten CD TÜT JW 72.1990). Rel. 1990. Jake Walton (Vocals, Guitar), Jo Partridge (Electric Guitar).
(The Lake Isle Of) Innisfree. Copyright © Jake Walton & Bucks Music Ltd. For Germany, Austria & Switzerland: Heupferd Musik Verlag GmbH. „Jake Walton – The Gloaming Grey" (Folkfreak LP FF 4001). Rec. & rel. 1979. Jake Walton (Guitar, Vocals). Rec. & rel. 1990. „Jake Walton – Songs From The Gurdy Man" (Wundertüte / Klangwelten CD TÜT JW 72.1990). Rel. 1990. Jake Walton (Vocals, Guitar), Eric Liorzou (Guitar), Jo Partridge (Electric Guitar). Stephen Cooney (Fretless Bass).
Gold And Silver. Copyright © Jake Walton & Bucks Music Ltd. For Germany, Austria & Switzerland: Heupferd Musik Verlag GmbH. „Jez Lowe & Jake Walton – Two A Roue" (Fellside Records LP FE 055). Rec. & rel. 1986. „Jake Walton – Songs From The Gurdy Man" (Wundertüte / Klangwelten CD TÜT JW 72.1990). Rel. 1990. Jake Walton (Vocals, Guitar), Jez Lowe (Vocals, Guitar).
Over Seal Sands. Copyright © Jez Lowe & Lowe Life Music. Rec. & rel. 2001 as bonus track on „Jez Lowe & Jake Walton – Two A Roue" (Tantobie Records TTRCD

101). Jez Lowe (Vocals, Keyboards, Whistle, Cittern), Jake Walton (Vocals, Hurdy Gurdy).
Beyond The Veil. Copyright © Jake Walton, Jez Lowe, Eric Liorzou & Bucks Music Ltd. Rec. 1998 – 1999. „Jake Walton – Emain" (Wundertüte CD TÜT 72.180). Rel. 2000. Jake Walton (Vocals, Hurdy Gurdy), Eric Liorzou (Mandola, Guitar).
Into The Twilight. Copyright © Jake Walton & Bucks Music Ltd. Rec. 1998 – 1999. „Jake Walton – Emain" (Wundertüte CD TÜT 72.180). Rel. 2000. Jake Walton (Guitar, Vocals), Eric Liorzou (Guitars), Erwan Volant (Bass Guitar), Jez Lowe (Harmony Vocals).
The Vagabond. Copyright © Jake Walton & Bucks Music Ltd. For Germany, Austria & Switzerland: Heupferd Musik Verlag GmbH. Rel. „Jake Walton – Sunlight And Shade" (Folfreak LP FF 4012). Rec. 1982, rel. 1983. Jake Walton (Guitar, Vocals). „Jake Walton – Songs From The Gurdy Man" (Wundertüte / Klangwelten CD TÜT JW 72.1990). Rel. 1990. Jake Walton (Vocals, Guitar), Eric Liorzou (Rhythm- & Lead-Guitar), Stephen Cooney (Bass).
Celtic Benediction. Copyright © Jake Walton & Bucks Music Ltd. For Germany, Austria & Switzerland: Heupferd Musik Verlag GmbH. Rel. „Jake Walton – Sunlight And Shade" (Folfreak LP FF 4012). Rec. 1982, rel. 1983. Jake Walton (Hurdy Gurdy, Vocals). „Jake Walton – Songs From The Gurdy Man" (Wundertüte / Klangwelten CD TÜT JW 72.1990). Rel. 1990 Jake Walton (Vocals, Hurdy Gurdy, Guitar). Eric Liorzou (Guitar), Stephen Cooney (Bass).
Emain. Copyright © Jake Walton & Bucks Music Ltd. „Jake Walton – Emain" (Wundertüte CD TÜT 72.180). Rec. 1998 – 1999, rel. 2000. Jake Walton (Guitar, Vocals), Eric Liorzou (Guitars, Low vocal harmony).
Lyric. Copyright © Mary Stewart,, Jake Walton & Bucks Music Ltd. „Jake Walton – Emain" (Wundertüte CD TÜT 72.180), Rec. 1998 – 1999, rel. 2000. Jake Walton (Guitar, Vocals), Eric Liorzou (Guitars), Erwan Volant (Bass Guitar).
Appleby Gallop. Copyright © Jake Walton, Jez Lowe & Low Life Music. Rec. & rel. 2001. „Jez Lowe & Jake Walton – Two A Roue" (Tantobie Records TTRCD 101). Jake Walton (Hurdy Gurdy), Jez Lowe (Cittern, Guitar), Paul Reeve (Percussion).
The Spinning Of The Wheel. Copyright © Jake Walton, Jez Lowe & Lowe Life Music.Rec. & rel. 2001. „Jez Lowe & Jake Walton – Two A Roue" (Tantobie Records TTRCD 101). Jake Walton (Dulcimer, Vocals), Jez Lowe (Cittern, Keyboards, Whistle, Vocals).
Silver Muse. Copyright © Jake Walton & Bucks Music Ltd.
By The Margin Of The Great Deep. Copyright words © George Russell, music © Jake Walton & Bucks Music Ltd.
The Plain Of Silver. Copyright © Jake Walton, Eric Liorzou & Bucks Music Ltd. Rec. „Jake Walton - Emain" (Wundertüte CD TÜT 72.180). Rec. 1998 – 1999. rel. 2000. Jake Walton (Hurdy Gurdy, Vocals), Eric Liorzou (Guitar, Mandola).
Peat Fire. Copyright words © John Klett, music © Jake Walton & Bucks Music Ltd. „Jake Walton – Emain" (Wundertüte CD TÜT 72.180). Rec. 1998 – 1999.rel. 2000. Jake Walton (Guitar, Vocals), Eric Liorzou (Guitar, Mandola).
Tom O'Bedlams's Dream. Copyright © Jake Walton & Bucks Music Ltd.
White Wave Sea. Copyright © Jake Walton & Bucks Music Ltd.

Discography Jake Walton

Jake Walton – The Gloaming Grey (Folk Freak LP FF 4001). Jake Walton – Sunlight And Shade (Folk Freak LP FF 4012). Jez Lowe & Jake Walton – Two A Roue (Fellside LP FE 055). „Jez Lowe & Jake Walton – Two A Roue" (Tantobie Records TTRCD 101). Jake Walton – Songs From The Gurdy Man (Wundertüte / Klangwelten CD TÜT JW 72.1990). Jake Walton – Emain (Wundertüte CD TÜT 72.180). Jake Walton – Silver Muse (Celtic Monkey CD CM 0001).

**As time goes by
Jez Lowe & Jake Walton 1986**

For more information visit
**www.jakewaltonmusic.co.uk
www.heupferd-musik.de/jake_walton.html**

Tabulaturen / Chord Shapes

(To be used with alternative guitar tunings)

DADGAD

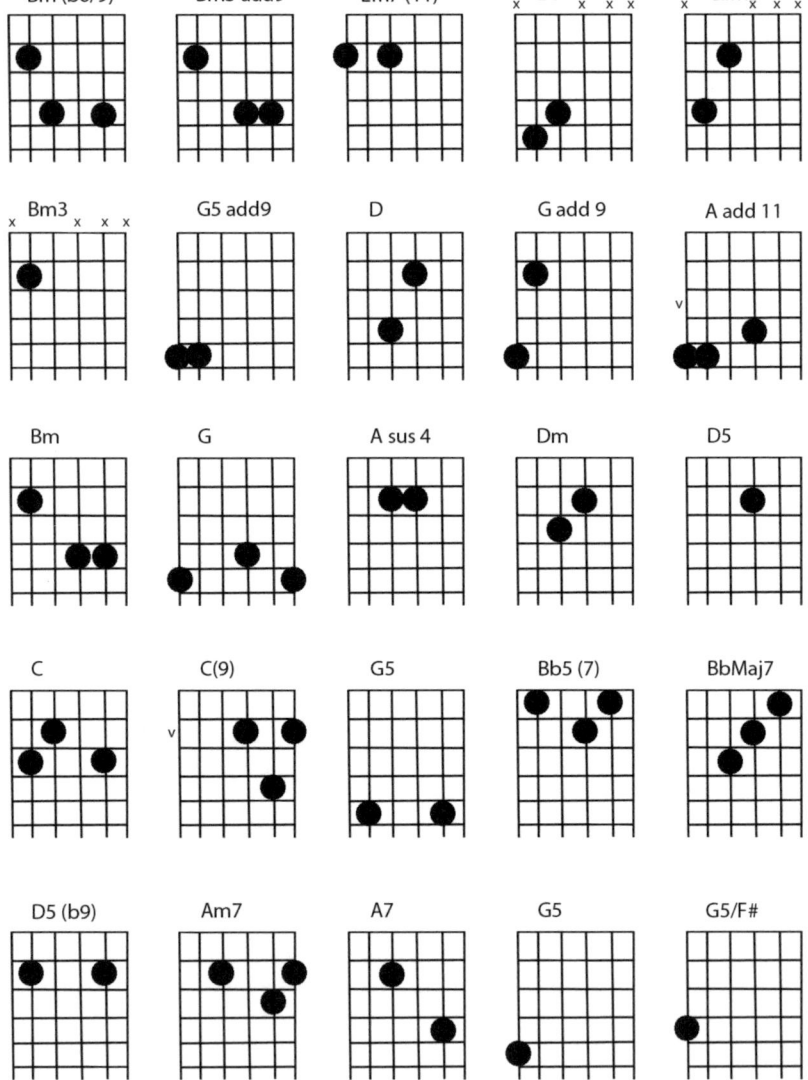

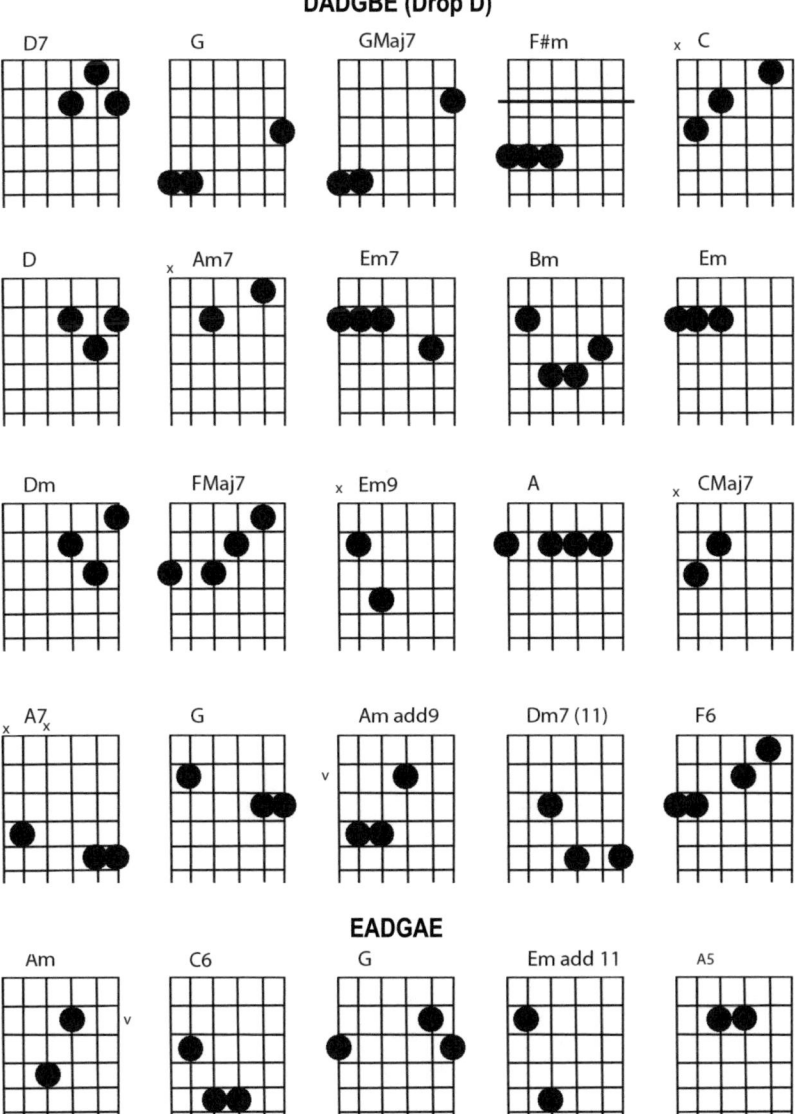

DADGBE (Drop D)

D7   G   GMaj7   F#m   x C

D   x Am7   Em7   Bm   Em

Dm   FMaj7   x Em9   A   x CMaj7

x A7 x   G   Am add9   Dm7 (11)   F6

EADGAE

Am   C6   G   Em add 11   A5

EADGAE

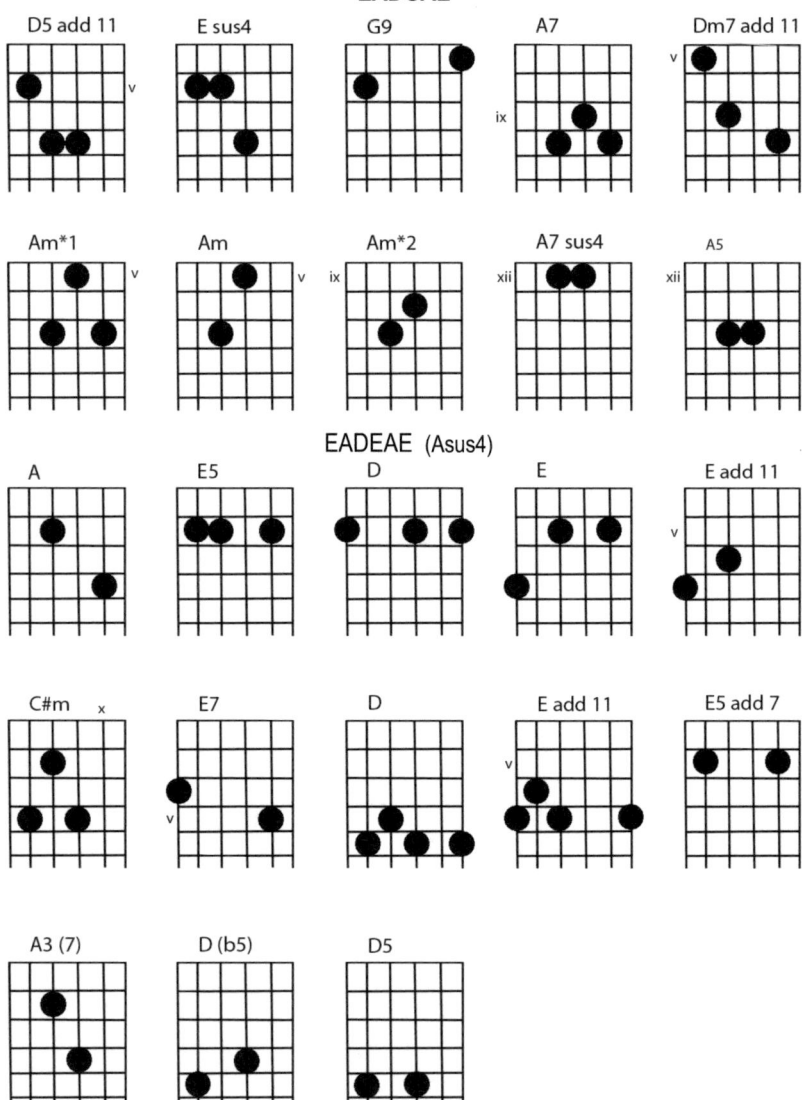

D5 add 11 · E sus4 · G9 · A7 · Dm7 add 11

Am*1 · Am · Am*2 · A7 sus4 · A5

EADEAE (Asus4)

A · E5 · D · E · E add 11

C#m · E7 · D · E add 11 · E5 add 7

A3 (7) · D (b5) · D5

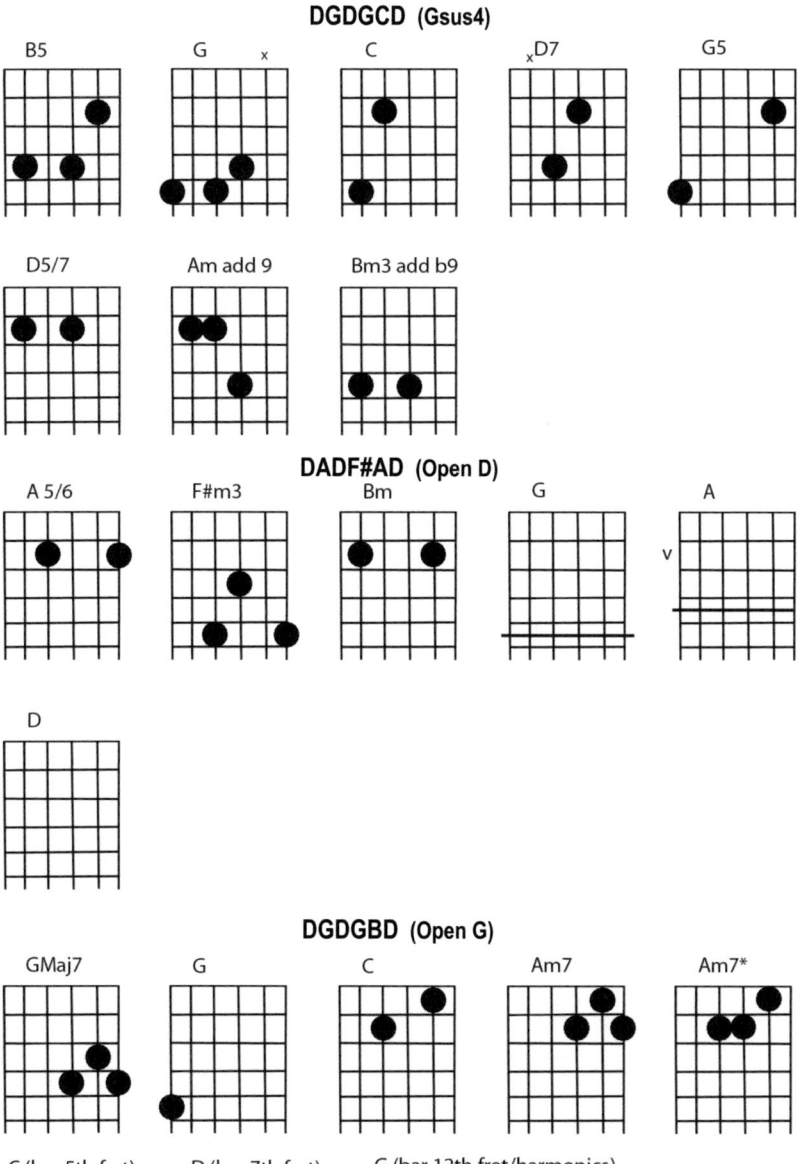

Das Klingt Gut!
Musik der Welt im Netz

Acoustic Music | Derroll Adams | Alla Turca | Anti-Hits
Balladen | Bastardmusik | Barden | Beatles 1968
Böhmische Harfe | Bordun | Pit Budde | Robert Burns
Guy Carawan | Cochise | Tom Daun | Ethnobeats
Flamenco | Folk Friends | Folkjazz | Folkmusic | Folkrock
Folksong | Dick Gaughan | Guru Guru | Mike Hanrahan
Harfenflocken | Harfissimo | Havana | Hobomusic
Bobby Holcomb | Annie Humphrey | Hurdy Gurdy
Indian Summer Sounds | Inti Illimani Histórico
Andy Irvine | Jams | Jazz | Wizz Jones | Klassikfolk
Kurt Klose | Jorge La Guardia | Lady's Voice | La Rotta
Latinpop | Latinjazz | Latinrap | Andreas Lieberg
Lovesongs | Denise M'Baye | Magic Irish Music
Magic Southsea | Migration & Musik | Noten
Protestsong | Rüdiger Oppermann | Marc Robine
Rootsmusic | Samba | Salsa | Son | Songbooks
Song Bücherei | Songwriter | Andy M. Stewart
Wolfgang Stute | Summit | Tierra | Trio Grande
Can Tufan | Jake Walton | Worldmusic

www.heupferd-musik.de